Network Security Protocols: IPsec, SSL/TLS, DTLS and More

James Relington

DEDICATION

To those who seek knowledge, inspiration, and new perspectives—
may this book be a companion on your journey, a spark for curiosity,
and a reminder that every page turned is a step toward discovery.

AKNOWLEDGEMENTS

I would like to express my deepest gratitude to everyone who contributed to the creation of this book. To my colleagues and mentors, your insights and expertise have been invaluable. A special thank you to my family and friends for their unwavering support and encouragement throughout this journey.

Introduction to Network Security

Network security is a critical aspect of modern digital infrastructure, underpinning the safe and reliable exchange of information across connected systems. As global dependence on the internet and networked devices continues to grow, so too does the need to protect data from unauthorized access, manipulation, and destruction. Network security encompasses the policies, procedures, and technologies designed to safeguard the integrity, confidentiality, and availability of data as it travels across or resides on network systems. In an age where cyber threats are constantly evolving, understanding the foundational concepts of network security is essential for any organization or individual seeking to protect their digital assets.

At its core, network security seeks to ensure that communication between users, systems, and services occurs in a secure and trustworthy environment. This is achieved by employing a range of technologies and techniques to prevent, detect, and respond to security threats. These threats can come in many forms, including malicious software, phishing attacks, denial-of-service attempts, data breaches, and insider threats. To counter these risks, network security strategies are built around key principles such as authentication, encryption, access control, and monitoring.

Authentication is the process of verifying the identity of users or systems before granting access to resources. This step is crucial in establishing trust between communicating parties. Techniques like passwords, digital certificates, biometrics, and multifactor authentication help ensure that only authorized entities can access sensitive information. Alongside authentication, encryption plays a vital role in maintaining confidentiality. By converting plaintext data into unreadable ciphertext, encryption protects information from being intercepted or understood by unauthorized actors during transmission or storage.

Access control mechanisms are used to enforce rules about who can access what resources under which conditions. These mechanisms are often implemented using firewalls, routers, and switches configured with security policies. Access control lists, role-based access control, and network segmentation are just some of the techniques used to limit exposure and minimize the risk of unauthorized access. Together with intrusion detection and prevention systems, these components form the foundation of a robust security architecture.

Monitoring and logging are equally important elements of network security. By constantly observing traffic patterns, system behaviors, and user activities, security professionals can identify anomalies that may indicate a breach or attempted attack. Security information and event management (SIEM) systems are commonly used to aggregate and analyze logs from various sources, providing real-time insights and historical data to support forensic investigations. The ability to quickly detect and respond to incidents can significantly reduce the impact of security breaches.

Network security is not a one-time effort, but rather a continuous process of assessment, improvement, and adaptation. New vulnerabilities are discovered regularly, and threat actors are constantly devising more sophisticated techniques. As such, security must be integrated into every phase of network design and maintenance. This includes selecting secure protocols, updating software and firmware regularly, and educating users on best practices. Human error remains one of the leading causes of security incidents, which makes training and awareness programs a vital part of any security strategy.

The scope of network security extends beyond traditional enterprise environments. With the rise of cloud computing, remote work, mobile devices, and the Internet of Things (IoT), the attack surface has expanded dramatically. Each connected device and service presents a potential entry point for attackers, requiring security controls to be applied consistently across heterogeneous environments. Technologies such as virtual private networks (VPNs), endpoint protection, and cloud access security brokers help address these challenges by extending the reach of security policies beyond the corporate perimeter.

The evolution of cyber threats has also led to the development of more advanced defense strategies. Concepts such as zero trust architecture, which assumes no implicit trust in users or devices regardless of location, are reshaping how organizations think about network security. Rather than relying on a strong perimeter, zero trust emphasizes continuous verification, least-privilege access, and micro-segmentation. This model is particularly effective in environments with distributed workforces and dynamic workloads.

Another important aspect of network security is compliance with legal and regulatory frameworks. Organizations are often required to adhere to standards such as the General Data Protection Regulation (GDPR), the Health Insurance Portability and Accountability Act (HIPAA), and the Payment Card Industry Data Security Standard (PCI DSS). These regulations set requirements for data protection and privacy, imposing penalties for non-compliance. Ensuring that network security practices align with regulatory mandates is essential for avoiding legal repercussions and maintaining customer trust.

Investing in network security also makes good business sense. The financial and reputational damage caused by a security breach can be devastating. Loss of customer data, intellectual property theft, operational disruptions, and legal liabilities are just a few of the potential consequences. By implementing effective security measures, organizations not only protect their assets but also enhance their resilience, competitiveness, and credibility in the marketplace.

In the broader context of national and international security, network protection is becoming a matter of strategic importance. Governments and critical infrastructure providers are frequent targets of cyber attacks aimed at espionage, sabotage, and disruption. As a result, there is growing collaboration between public and private sectors to share threat intelligence, develop standards, and respond to cyber incidents. The future of network security will likely involve greater use of artificial intelligence, machine learning, and automation to keep pace with the scale and speed of modern threats.

Ultimately, network security is a multifaceted discipline that touches every aspect of digital life. From protecting personal communications to securing global financial systems, the importance of maintaining trust in networked environments cannot be overstated. As technology continues to advance, so too must our efforts to defend it. By understanding the principles, challenges, and tools of network security, individuals and organizations alike can contribute to a safer and more secure digital world.

Fundamentals of Cryptography

Cryptography is the science and art of securing information by transforming it into a format that is unintelligible to unauthorized parties. This transformation process relies on mathematical techniques that ensure confidentiality, integrity, authenticity, and non-repudiation of data. In a world increasingly driven by digital communication, financial transactions, and cloud-based services, cryptography plays a crucial role in protecting information from malicious actors and ensuring privacy. Understanding the fundamentals of cryptography involves exploring its key principles, types, historical context, and modern applications, as well as the algorithms that power secure systems today.

The origins of cryptography can be traced back thousands of years, to times when military and political leaders needed to protect sensitive information. Ancient civilizations such as the Egyptians and Romans developed early cryptographic methods, like the Caesar cipher, to conceal messages. These early techniques often relied on simple substitution or transposition, and while they were effective for their time, they could be broken with relative ease by skilled adversaries. The advent of the digital age has transformed cryptography into a highly sophisticated discipline grounded in complex mathematical theory and computer science.

At its core, cryptography involves two main processes: encryption and decryption. Encryption is the method of converting plaintext (readable data) into ciphertext (unreadable data) using an algorithm and a key. The key is a piece of information that determines the output of the cryptographic process. Decryption is the reverse process, converting ciphertext back into plaintext using the appropriate key. The strength of modern cryptography lies in its ability to make decryption practically impossible without the correct key, even when the encryption algorithm is publicly known.

There are two major types of cryptographic systems: symmetric-key cryptography and asymmetric-key cryptography. In symmetric-key systems, the same key is used for both encryption and decryption. This approach is efficient and fast, making it suitable for encrypting large volumes of data. However, the main challenge is key distribution: both parties must securely exchange the secret key before communication begins. If the key is intercepted, the entire system is compromised. Common symmetric algorithms include AES (Advanced Encryption Standard) and DES (Data Encryption Standard), with AES being widely adopted due to its robustness and efficiency.

Asymmetric-key cryptography, also known as public-key cryptography, addresses the key distribution problem by using a pair of keys: a public key and a private key. The public key is shared openly, while the private key remains confidential. Data encrypted with the public key can only be decrypted with the corresponding private key, and vice versa. This system allows secure communication between parties who have never met before, as there is no need to exchange a secret key beforehand. Asymmetric cryptography also enables digital signatures, which verify the authenticity and integrity of messages. Notable algorithms in this domain include RSA (Rivest-Shamir-Adleman), ECC (Elliptic Curve Cryptography), and Diffie-Hellman key exchange.

A central concept in cryptography is the idea of computational hardness. A cryptographic algorithm is considered secure if the effort required to break it exceeds the resources (time, memory, computing power) available to an attacker. For example, brute-force attacks that try every possible key combination become infeasible as key lengths increase. This is why modern encryption standards use keys of at least 128 bits, with many applications using 256-bit keys for higher security. However, the evolving capabilities of adversaries, especially with the potential rise of quantum computing, continue to challenge the assumptions of current cryptographic systems.

Another fundamental aspect of cryptography is the use of cryptographic hash functions. Unlike encryption algorithms, hash functions take an input and produce a fixed-size output, called a hash or digest, that cannot be reversed to obtain the original input. These functions are crucial in verifying data integrity, storing passwords securely, and building digital signatures. A good hash function must be collision-resistant, meaning it should be extremely difficult to find two different inputs that produce the same hash output. Popular cryptographic hash functions include SHA-256 (Secure Hash Algorithm 256-bit) and SHA-3, both widely used in blockchain technologies and secure communications.

Authentication and non-repudiation are also essential components of cryptographic systems. Authentication ensures that the parties involved in a communication are who they claim to be, often using digital certificates and public key infrastructures (PKI). Non-repudiation guarantees that a sender cannot deny having sent a message, thanks to the verifiable evidence provided by digital signatures. Together, these elements build trust in digital interactions, enabling secure e-commerce, confidential email communication, and safe software updates.

Cryptography is not without its challenges. One major concern is the management of cryptographic keys. Keys must be generated, distributed, stored, and eventually destroyed in a secure manner. If a private key is lost or stolen, the entire cryptographic system can be rendered ineffective. Furthermore, vulnerabilities in software implementation, user behavior, or side-channel attacks can undermine even the most secure cryptographic algorithms. Thus, cryptographic systems must be designed with both theoretical soundness and practical considerations in mind.

The field of cryptography continues to evolve rapidly, driven by the demands of cybersecurity, digital transformation, and emerging technologies. Quantum cryptography, which leverages principles of quantum mechanics to secure data, promises a new frontier in information security. Post-quantum cryptography, meanwhile, seeks to develop classical algorithms that remain secure against quantum attacks. These advancements highlight the dynamic nature of the field and its vital importance in safeguarding digital life.

Understanding the fundamentals of cryptography provides the foundation for designing, analyzing, and implementing secure systems. From securing personal data on smartphones to protecting global financial networks, cryptography underpins the trust that modern society places in digital technology. As the world becomes increasingly interconnected and reliant on information systems, the role of cryptography will only grow more central and indispensable.

Authentication, Integrity, and Confidentiality

Authentication, integrity, and confidentiality are the foundational pillars of information security. These three principles work together to ensure that data is protected from unauthorized access, alteration, and disclosure. As digital communication, online services, and interconnected systems have become a fundamental part of everyday life, the importance of securing digital assets and communication channels has grown exponentially. Whether transmitting a simple message between two individuals or conducting a large-scale financial transaction, these three core concepts are critical in maintaining trust, reliability, and privacy in cyberspace.

Authentication is the process of verifying the identity of a user, device, or system. It ensures that an entity is who or what it claims to be. Without reliable authentication mechanisms, any user could gain access to sensitive data or systems simply by pretending to be someone else. Traditionally, authentication has been implemented through usernames and passwords, but as threats have evolved, so too have authentication methods. Today, more robust systems include multi-factor authentication, which combines something the user knows (like a password), something the user has (like a smartphone or security token), and something the user is (such as a fingerprint or facial recognition). These techniques aim to minimize the chances of impersonation or unauthorized access.

Authentication is not limited to individuals. Systems, applications, and devices also need to authenticate themselves to one another. For instance, when you visit a secure website, your browser verifies the site's digital certificate to ensure that it is indeed the site it claims to be. This process, part of the SSL/TLS protocol, prevents attackers from tricking users into connecting to malicious sites that pose as legitimate ones. Authentication is the first line of defense in any secure communication, and without it, there is no way to establish trust between communicating parties.

Once authentication is established, the next critical concept is integrity. Integrity refers to the assurance that data has not been altered in an unauthorized or undetected manner. This means that the content of a message or a file remains the same from the time it was created or sent until it is received or accessed. If an attacker were to intercept and modify a message in transit, the system must be able to detect this tampering. Maintaining integrity is essential not only for communication but also for stored data, ensuring that records, files, or databases have not been corrupted or maliciously changed.

To ensure data integrity, cryptographic hash functions are commonly used. These functions take input data and produce a fixed-size string of characters known as a hash value or digest. If even a single bit of the original data changes, the resulting hash will be completely different. This property makes hash functions ideal for detecting tampering. Digital signatures, which combine hashing with asymmetric encryption, allow recipients to verify both the origin and integrity of a message. When a sender digitally signs a message, they create a hash of the message and encrypt it with their private key. The recipient can then use the sender's public key to decrypt the hash and compare it with a freshly computed hash of the received message. If the values match, the data has not been altered and the sender is authenticated.

Confidentiality is the third essential pillar of information security. It involves protecting information from unauthorized access and disclosure. In simple terms, confidentiality ensures that only those who are authorized to view or use certain data are able to do so. This principle is most commonly implemented through encryption. Encryption transforms readable data into an unreadable format using an algorithm and a cryptographic key. Only those with the correct key can decrypt the data and access its original form. This protects sensitive information such as personal data, financial records, or classified documents from being exposed to unauthorized users.

Confidentiality is crucial in a wide range of contexts, from private communications between individuals to the protection of trade secrets and national security information. Even in less obvious cases, such as everyday use of cloud storage or messaging apps, confidentiality ensures that data remains private and inaccessible to eavesdroppers or hackers. Strong encryption protocols, secure key management, and access control mechanisms are all necessary to enforce confidentiality in digital environments. Without these protections, even the most robust authentication and integrity systems would fall short of securing sensitive information.

The interplay between authentication, integrity, and confidentiality creates a comprehensive security framework. Each element addresses a different aspect of information protection, but none is sufficient on its own. For example, encrypted communication ensures confidentiality, but without authentication, there is no way to be sure that the encrypted message came from a legitimate source. Similarly, if a message is received from a verified sender but the content has been tampered with, integrity has been compromised. All three principles must work in harmony to achieve true data security.

In practice, implementing these principles often involves a combination of technologies and protocols. For example, the HTTPS protocol used in web browsing combines authentication through digital certificates, confidentiality through encryption, and integrity through message authentication codes. Secure email systems use digital signatures and encryption to ensure that messages are authentic, untampered, and private. Virtual private networks (VPNs) rely on these principles to protect data transmitted over public networks. Each of these applications demonstrates how authentication, integrity, and confidentiality are applied to real-world problems and scenarios.

As the complexity of digital systems increases and cyber threats become more sophisticated, maintaining strong authentication, integrity, and confidentiality becomes even more critical. The rise of artificial intelligence, the Internet of Things, and cloud computing has introduced new challenges in securing identities, data, and communication channels. Adversaries constantly seek to exploit weaknesses in authentication protocols, intercept unprotected data, or manipulate information to serve malicious purposes. For this reason, organizations and individuals must remain vigilant and proactive in applying best practices for securing their digital environments.

Understanding and applying the principles of authentication, integrity, and confidentiality is essential for anyone involved in managing or using information systems. These concepts form the backbone of cybersecurity and are integral to the safe operation of digital technologies across industries and sectors. Whether safeguarding personal data, corporate secrets, or national infrastructure, these three pillars provide the structure necessary for trust and reliability in the digital age.

Symmetric vs Asymmetric Encryption

Encryption is a vital component of modern cybersecurity, allowing individuals, organizations, and governments to protect sensitive data from unauthorized access. Two main categories of encryption are used in digital security: symmetric and asymmetric encryption. Both methods serve the fundamental purpose of transforming readable data, known as plaintext, into an unreadable format called ciphertext. However, they differ in how they achieve this transformation and in the specific use cases they are best suited for. Understanding the distinction between symmetric and asymmetric encryption is essential for grasping how secure communication, authentication, and digital privacy function in today's interconnected world.

Symmetric encryption is the older and more traditional of the two. It relies on a single shared key for both encryption and decryption. This means that the same key used to encode the message must also be used by the recipient to decode it. The simplicity of this model is one of its greatest strengths, as symmetric encryption is generally faster and more efficient than its asymmetric counterpart. Because it requires less computational power, it is ideal for encrypting large amounts of data quickly. For this reason, symmetric algorithms are widely used in applications such as securing stored data, encrypting files on a hard drive, or protecting communication in real-time systems like video conferencing or streaming.

One of the most well-known symmetric encryption algorithms is the Advanced Encryption Standard, or AES. It has become a global standard due to its strong security and efficiency. AES can use key sizes of 128, 192, or 256 bits, with longer keys offering greater resistance to brute-force attacks. Another example of a symmetric cipher is DES, the Data Encryption Standard, which was widely used in the past but is now considered obsolete due to its relatively short key length and vulnerability to modern computing power. Despite their strengths, symmetric systems face a significant challenge: the secure distribution of the key. Since both the sender and the recipient must have access to the same key, they must find a safe way to exchange it. If the key is intercepted during transmission, an attacker could decrypt all future communications encrypted with that key.

To overcome the limitations of key distribution in symmetric encryption, asymmetric encryption was developed. Also known as public-key cryptography, asymmetric encryption uses two different keys: a public key and a private key. The public key can be shared openly, while the private key must be kept secret. When someone wants to send an encrypted message, they use the recipient's public key to encrypt it. Only the recipient, who holds the corresponding private key, can decrypt the message. This approach eliminates the need for secure key exchange, as there is no risk in making the public key widely available.

One of the most widely used asymmetric algorithms is RSA, named after its inventors Rivest, Shamir, and Adleman. RSA's security is based on the mathematical difficulty of factoring large prime numbers.

Another prominent example is Elliptic Curve Cryptography, or ECC, which achieves the same level of security as RSA with much smaller key sizes, making it more efficient for devices with limited resources such as smartphones or embedded systems. Asymmetric encryption also enables digital signatures, which allow the sender of a message to prove their identity and ensure that the message has not been altered. This is achieved by creating a cryptographic hash of the message and encrypting it with the sender's private key. The recipient can then verify the signature by decrypting it with the sender's public key and comparing it to a newly generated hash of the message.

Despite its strengths, asymmetric encryption is not without drawbacks. It is significantly slower than symmetric encryption, especially when processing large amounts of data. The mathematical operations required for asymmetric encryption are more complex, making it less efficient for tasks that demand high speed or low latency. For this reason, asymmetric encryption is often used in combination with symmetric encryption in a process known as hybrid encryption. In a hybrid system, asymmetric encryption is used to securely exchange a symmetric key, and then the symmetric key is used to encrypt the actual data. This approach leverages the strengths of both methods while minimizing their weaknesses.

The coexistence of symmetric and asymmetric encryption in real-world applications highlights the importance of understanding both approaches. For example, when you access a secure website via HTTPS, your browser uses asymmetric encryption to authenticate the website and exchange a symmetric session key. Once the key is exchanged, all subsequent data transferred between your browser and the website is encrypted using symmetric encryption. This model provides both secure key exchange and high-performance data transfer.

Choosing between symmetric and asymmetric encryption depends on the specific needs of the system or application. If speed and efficiency are critical, such as in encrypting large files or securing real-time communications, symmetric encryption is typically the better choice. If secure key exchange, identity verification, or digital signatures are required, then asymmetric encryption is more suitable. In many cases, a layered approach using both methods offers the most effective solution.

In today's digital ecosystem, where sensitive data is constantly being transmitted across global networks, encryption is more important than ever. The difference between symmetric and asymmetric encryption lies not in their goals but in the methods they use to achieve those goals. Both play a crucial role in ensuring secure communication, safeguarding personal and financial information, and building the trust necessary for online transactions. As technology continues to evolve and new threats emerge, so too will the algorithms and strategies used to protect our data, but the fundamental distinction between symmetric and asymmetric encryption will remain a cornerstone of modern cybersecurity.

Key Exchange Mechanisms

Key exchange mechanisms are fundamental to modern cryptography because they enable two or more parties to establish a shared secret over an insecure communication channel. Without an effective way to exchange cryptographic keys securely, encryption systems would fail to protect sensitive information from eavesdroppers or attackers. The primary goal of a key exchange protocol is to allow participants to agree upon a secret key without exposing it to anyone who might be monitoring the communication. Once the shared key is established, it can be used to encrypt and decrypt messages using symmetric encryption, which is faster and more efficient than asymmetric encryption for ongoing data transmission.

In early cryptographic systems, key exchange was a major weakness. Symmetric encryption systems require both parties to use the same secret key, which means the key had to be physically delivered or transmitted over a secure channel. This posed logistical and security challenges, especially when the parties were geographically distant. If the key was intercepted during transmission, the security of the entire communication would be compromised. The advent of asymmetric cryptography in the 1970s provided a new way to solve this problem, laying the foundation for secure key exchange over public networks.

One of the earliest and most influential key exchange mechanisms is the Diffie-Hellman key exchange protocol, introduced in 1976 by

Whitfield Diffie and Martin Hellman. This protocol was revolutionary because it allowed two parties to create a shared secret over an insecure channel without actually exchanging the secret itself. The protocol is based on the mathematical difficulty of solving discrete logarithm problems in a finite field. Each party generates a private key and a corresponding public key derived from shared base values. They then exchange public keys and perform a mathematical operation using their private key and the other party's public key to compute the shared secret. Because of the mathematical properties of the algorithm, both parties arrive at the same secret without ever sending it directly.

Despite its elegance and utility, the original Diffie-Hellman protocol does not provide authentication, which means that it is vulnerable to man-in-the-middle attacks. In such an attack, an adversary intercepts the public keys exchanged between the two parties and substitutes them with their own. This allows the attacker to establish separate shared keys with both parties, decrypt and possibly alter messages, and then forward them along. To address this issue, variations of the protocol have been developed that incorporate authentication mechanisms, such as digital signatures or certificates issued by trusted authorities. These improvements ensure that each party can verify the identity of the other before agreeing on a key.

Another widely used key exchange mechanism is the RSA algorithm, which can be used both for encryption and key exchange. In the RSA key exchange process, one party generates a public-private key pair and shares the public key with the other party. The second party uses the public key to encrypt a randomly generated symmetric key and sends the encrypted key to the first party, who then decrypts it using their private key. This method ensures that only the intended recipient can derive the symmetric key, even if the communication is intercepted. RSA-based key exchange provides both confidentiality and authentication when combined with digital signatures and trusted certificate authorities.

Elliptic Curve Diffie-Hellman, or ECDH, is a modern variation of the traditional Diffie-Hellman protocol that uses the mathematics of elliptic curve cryptography. ECDH provides the same functionality as the original protocol but with significantly smaller key sizes, which results in faster computations and reduced storage requirements. This makes ECDH especially attractive for devices with limited processing power, such as smartphones, smart cards, and Internet of Things devices. The efficiency of ECDH has led to its adoption in a wide range of secure communication protocols, including the TLS protocol used in HTTPS.

Key exchange mechanisms are often integrated into larger cryptographic protocols and systems. For example, the Transport Layer Security protocol, which secures communication over the internet, uses key exchange during the handshake phase to establish a secure session between the client and server. During this handshake, the server presents a digital certificate that contains its public key, and the client uses this key to securely transmit a symmetric session key. Once the session key is established, both parties use symmetric encryption for the remainder of the communication, benefiting from both the strong security of asymmetric encryption and the speed of symmetric encryption.

In many real-world systems, hybrid key exchange methods are employed. These methods combine the strengths of both asymmetric and symmetric cryptography. The asymmetric portion is used only at the beginning of the communication session to exchange keys securely, while the symmetric portion is used afterward to encrypt data efficiently. This hybrid approach is a practical solution to the performance limitations of asymmetric algorithms and ensures strong security throughout the communication process.

The security of key exchange mechanisms depends heavily on the strength of the underlying mathematical problems. For instance, the security of Diffie-Hellman and RSA relies on the difficulty of factoring large integers or computing discrete logarithms. However, advances in quantum computing could threaten these foundations. Algorithms like Shor's algorithm theoretically enable quantum computers to solve these problems much faster than classical computers, potentially rendering current key exchange protocols vulnerable. In response, researchers are developing post-quantum key exchange algorithms that rely on mathematical problems believed to be resistant to quantum attacks, such as lattice-based or code-based cryptography.

Despite technological advances and new threats, key exchange mechanisms remain central to secure digital communication. Whether securing emails, online banking, cloud storage, or instant messaging, these protocols ensure that sensitive data is protected from unauthorized access by enabling parties to establish shared secrets in a hostile environment. The continued development and refinement of key exchange methods reflect the ongoing need to adapt to changing technology while maintaining the fundamental principles of privacy and security in the digital world.

Introduction to Network Protocols

Network protocols are the essential rules and conventions that govern how devices communicate across a network. Without these protocols, it would be impossible for different systems, often built by different manufacturers and using different software, to exchange information in a consistent and reliable way. From sending a simple email to streaming a video or accessing a website, every action on the internet or a local network relies on these protocols functioning smoothly. They define how data is formatted, transmitted, compressed, routed, and verified, making them the invisible backbone of all digital communication.

The internet, as we know it, is a vast and complex network of networks, with billions of devices interacting constantly. Each device must follow strict procedures to ensure that data sent from one location reaches its correct destination, is interpreted accurately, and maintains its integrity throughout the journey. Network protocols enable this orchestration by setting standards that all participating devices agree to follow. These standards are not bound to any specific hardware or software, which is what makes the internet and other networks so flexible and scalable.

One of the most fundamental families of network protocols is the TCP/IP suite. The Transmission Control Protocol (TCP) and the Internet Protocol (IP) work together to ensure that data packets are reliably delivered across networks. IP is responsible for addressing and routing packets to their destination, while TCP manages the sequencing, retransmission of lost packets, and ensuring that data arrives intact and in the correct order. This separation of duties allows IP to function as a delivery mechanism, while TCP provides the reliability and error checking required by most applications. Another protocol, UDP or User Datagram Protocol, also uses IP but sacrifices reliability for speed, making it suitable for applications where real-time performance is more important than perfect delivery, such as voice over IP or online gaming.

Each layer in the TCP/IP model handles specific tasks and relies on the layers above and below it. For instance, the application layer includes protocols like HTTP for web browsing, FTP for file transfers, SMTP for sending email, and DNS for resolving domain names to IP addresses. These protocols define the structure and content of messages and determine how different software applications interact with the network. Below the application layer, the transport layer (including TCP and UDP) manages end-to-end communication between hosts. The internet layer handles addressing and routing, ensuring that packets find the most efficient path through the network. Finally, the link layer is responsible for communication within a local network segment, using technologies such as Ethernet or Wi-Fi.

HTTP, or Hypertext Transfer Protocol, is a cornerstone of the modern web. It allows browsers to request resources from web servers and receive responses in a structured format. Although HTTP is stateless and does not retain any memory of previous requests, newer versions such as HTTP/2 and HTTP/3 introduce features like multiplexing, header compression, and faster connection establishment to improve performance and efficiency. The secure version, HTTPS, incorporates SSL/TLS encryption to protect data in transit, ensuring confidentiality and integrity for sensitive communications like online banking or e-commerce transactions.

The Domain Name System, or DNS, is another critical protocol that acts as the internet's address book. Humans prefer to use readable names like example.com rather than numerical IP addresses. DNS translates these domain names into IP addresses so that browsers and other applications can locate the correct servers. The DNS process involves querying hierarchical servers that store records mapping domain names to IP addresses. This translation occurs behind the scenes every time a user accesses a website, clicks on a link, or sends an email.

Email communication is supported by several protocols working in tandem. SMTP, or Simple Mail Transfer Protocol, handles the sending of messages between servers. On the receiving end, protocols like IMAP (Internet Message Access Protocol) and POP3 (Post Office Protocol) allow users to retrieve their email. IMAP enables users to manage their emails on the server, providing synchronization across multiple devices, while POP3 downloads messages to a single device and typically deletes them from the server afterward.

Routing protocols play an equally vital role in ensuring that data finds its way through the vast web of networks that make up the internet. Protocols like OSPF (Open Shortest Path First) and BGP (Border Gateway Protocol) help routers determine the best path for forwarding packets. BGP, often referred to as the protocol that makes the internet work, is responsible for routing between different autonomous systems, such as internet service providers. These protocols dynamically adapt to changes in network topology, such as outages or congestion, to maintain efficient and reliable data flow.

Security protocols are also integral to modern networking. Protocols like IPsec provide secure communication over IP networks by encrypting and authenticating packets. TLS, or Transport Layer Security, is used to secure various application-layer protocols and ensure private communication over the internet. These protocols help prevent eavesdropping, data tampering, and impersonation, all of which are critical threats in an open and interconnected environment.

Network protocols are not static; they evolve over time to address emerging needs and threats. New versions are developed, older ones are deprecated, and extensions are added to improve efficiency, compatibility, or security. For example, IPv6 was introduced to replace IPv4, which is limited in the number of available addresses. IPv6 not only provides a vastly larger address space but also includes improvements in routing and configuration. The adoption of new protocols often takes time, as global infrastructure and legacy systems must be updated in a coordinated and backward-compatible manner.

Understanding network protocols is essential for anyone working in information technology, cybersecurity, software development, or systems administration. They provide the foundation upon which applications are built and ensure that devices, regardless of their origin, can communicate reliably and securely. As our reliance on digital communication continues to grow, so does the importance of the protocols that silently manage the complexity of networked systems. Every message sent, every file shared, and every webpage loaded is made possible by these carefully designed and meticulously implemented sets of rules.

The OSI Model and Security Layers

The OSI model, or Open Systems Interconnection model, is a conceptual framework used to understand and standardize the functions of a telecommunication or computing system without regard to its underlying internal structure and technology. Developed by the International Organization for Standardization, the OSI model divides the networking process into seven distinct layers. Each layer performs a specific role in the process of communication between systems, and together they form a comprehensive approach to understanding how data moves from one point to another across a network. Importantly, the OSI model also serves as a valuable reference for understanding how to implement security measures at different stages of network communication.

Beginning at the top, the application layer is the interface closest to the end user. It provides services directly to the software applications, enabling functions such as file transfers, email, and remote access. Security at this level often includes data encryption, authentication, and user-level access controls. Ensuring that applications follow secure coding practices and protocols like HTTPS or SFTP is essential to protect user data and prevent threats like buffer overflows, injection attacks, or session hijacking. The use of multifactor authentication, digital certificates, and secure application protocols helps safeguard communication between users and systems at the application layer.

The presentation layer is responsible for the translation, encryption, and compression of data. This is where data is formatted in a way that the application layer can understand, regardless of the differences in data representation among systems. One of the most crucial security functions at this layer is encryption. Secure communication protocols use encryption to protect sensitive information in transit. This layer ensures that data can only be interpreted by the intended recipient, preserving confidentiality. For example, when a user accesses a banking website, encryption at the presentation layer protects the information from being read by attackers, even if the communication is intercepted.

The session layer is responsible for establishing, maintaining, and terminating connections between devices. It manages sessions between computers and ensures that data streams remain separate and properly synchronized. Security at this layer involves session management controls, including timeouts, re-authentication, and protection against session hijacking. Attackers may attempt to exploit open or unprotected sessions to gain unauthorized access or impersonate legitimate users. Therefore, strong authentication mechanisms and monitoring for unusual session behavior are important strategies to secure this layer.

The transport layer provides end-to-end communication services for applications. It is responsible for error correction, data flow control, and data segmentation. Two key protocols operate at this layer: TCP, which provides reliable, connection-oriented communication, and UDP, which offers faster but less reliable communication. Security at the transport layer is vital for ensuring data integrity and reliability. Protocols like TLS operate here to provide encryption and secure session establishment. By ensuring that data packets are not altered or tampered with during transmission, the transport layer plays a critical role in maintaining the trustworthiness of network communications.

The network layer is responsible for logical addressing and routing. It determines how data is transferred between devices across multiple networks. The IP protocol functions at this layer, assigning unique addresses to each device on the network and directing data packets to their destination. Security at this layer involves protecting routing information and ensuring that packets are not diverted, dropped, or altered by malicious actors. Techniques such as IPsec help secure IP packets by providing authentication and encryption. Preventing route manipulation attacks like route injection or spoofing is crucial to maintaining a secure and stable network infrastructure.

The data link layer controls how data is packaged for transmission over physical media. It manages error detection and correction from the physical layer and ensures reliable point-to-point communication. It also defines protocols for media access and data framing. Security at the data link layer involves ensuring that devices on a local network can communicate without interference or eavesdropping. Attacks such as MAC address spoofing, ARP poisoning, and switch flooding target this layer. To defend against these threats, network administrators employ measures like port security, VLAN segmentation, and secure ARP implementations to control device access and prevent unauthorized communication.

The physical layer is the lowest layer of the OSI model and deals with the actual transmission of raw bits over a physical medium such as cables, radio frequencies, or fiber optics. This layer encompasses the hardware elements involved in networking, including cables, switches, routers, and network interface cards. Physical security is often overlooked but is just as important as logical security. Ensuring that networking hardware is protected from tampering or unauthorized access is essential. Techniques to secure this layer include locking network equipment in secured cabinets, restricting physical access to networking environments, and employing surveillance and monitoring to detect potential threats.

The layered structure of the OSI model allows for a clear understanding of where specific security mechanisms should be applied. Each layer has unique responsibilities and vulnerabilities, and therefore, each layer requires its own set of protective measures. Security that is too heavily focused on a single layer creates vulnerabilities elsewhere. A comprehensive security strategy, often referred to as defense in depth, involves implementing safeguards across all layers. This redundancy ensures that even if one layer is compromised, others can provide continued protection.

The OSI model not only aids in understanding how data is transmitted but also serves as a guide for developing secure systems and networks. It helps professionals identify weak points in communication processes and design solutions tailored to each layer's specific needs. For example, a breach in the transport layer might prompt administrators to review TLS configurations, while persistent session hijacking issues may require improvements at the session or application layers. Likewise, anomalies in routing behavior might signal manipulation at the network layer, requiring IPsec deployment or deeper traffic analysis.

In today's cybersecurity landscape, threats continue to evolve, targeting not only software vulnerabilities but also network protocols and hardware. Understanding the OSI model equips cybersecurity professionals, network administrators, and developers with the framework needed to analyze complex systems and implement multi-layered defenses. Whether the concern is protecting confidential data, preventing unauthorized access, or maintaining system integrity, the OSI model provides a valuable structure for aligning technical defenses with organizational security goals. By approaching network security through the lens of the OSI model, one can build resilient systems capable of withstanding the increasingly sophisticated threats that exist in a hyper-connected world.

Threats in Modern Network Environments

Modern network environments are more complex and interconnected than ever before, creating a fertile ground for a wide variety of security threats. With the rapid expansion of cloud computing, mobile devices, remote work, and Internet of Things technologies, the attack surface of organizations and individuals has grown exponentially. Threats in today's networks are no longer limited to simple malware or email phishing; they now include highly sophisticated and targeted attacks that often go unnoticed until the damage has already been done. Understanding the nature of these threats is crucial for building effective defense mechanisms and maintaining the integrity, confidentiality, and availability of networked systems.

One of the most persistent and damaging threats in modern networks is ransomware. Ransomware attacks involve malicious software that encrypts a victim's data and demands payment, often in cryptocurrency, to restore access. These attacks can cripple entire organizations by locking access to critical data and systems. In many cases, even if the ransom is paid, there is no guarantee that the data will be recovered or that the attacker has not already exfiltrated sensitive information. Ransomware has evolved to target not only individual computers but also entire networks, exploiting vulnerabilities in unpatched systems and using lateral movement to spread across internal environments. High-profile incidents affecting hospitals, municipalities, and multinational companies highlight how devastating these attacks can be.

Another serious concern is the threat of phishing and social engineering. These attacks target the human element of cybersecurity, tricking users into revealing credentials, clicking on malicious links, or downloading infected files. Attackers often disguise themselves as legitimate institutions, such as banks or government agencies, to deceive their targets. Phishing emails have grown more convincing with the use of real logos, spoofed addresses, and personalized content, making it increasingly difficult for users to detect fraud. In corporate environments, spear phishing targets specific individuals with tailored messages designed to exploit their roles or access privileges. Once access is gained, attackers may move laterally through the network, escalate privileges, or exfiltrate sensitive data.

Distributed denial-of-service (DDoS) attacks are also a growing threat to modern networks. In a DDoS attack, a network or service is flooded with a massive volume of traffic from multiple sources, overwhelming its resources and rendering it unavailable to legitimate users. These attacks can last for minutes or days and may be used as a smokescreen for other malicious activities such as data breaches. DDoS attacks have become more powerful with the rise of botnets composed of compromised IoT devices, which can be exploited due to weak security configurations. Attackers may also use amplification techniques to magnify the impact of their traffic, making even small botnets capable of significant disruption.

Advanced persistent threats, or APTs, represent one of the most sophisticated forms of attack. Unlike opportunistic attacks that target random victims, APTs are carried out by highly skilled and often state-sponsored groups with specific objectives, such as espionage, intellectual property theft, or disruption of critical infrastructure. These attackers infiltrate a network and remain undetected for extended periods, quietly collecting information or manipulating systems. APTs often employ a range of tactics, including spear phishing, zero-day vulnerabilities, and custom malware, and their persistence makes them particularly difficult to detect and eradicate. Organizations targeted by APTs face significant risks, not only in terms of data loss but also reputational damage and regulatory consequences.

Insider threats continue to pose a major challenge in network environments. These threats originate from individuals within the organization who misuse their access to steal information, sabotage systems, or leak sensitive data. Insider threats can be malicious, such as a disgruntled employee intentionally harming the company, or unintentional, such as a well-meaning staff member falling for a phishing scam or mishandling sensitive files. The complexity of modern networks and the widespread use of cloud services make it more difficult to monitor and control insider activities. Effective mitigation requires a combination of access controls, user behavior analytics, and a strong security culture supported by training and awareness programs.

Man-in-the-middle attacks are another threat that targets communication channels. In these attacks, a malicious actor intercepts and potentially alters the communication between two parties without their knowledge. By positioning themselves between the sender and recipient, the attacker can eavesdrop on conversations, steal login credentials, or inject malicious content. These attacks are especially dangerous on unsecured or public networks, such as open Wi-Fi hotspots. Protocols like HTTPS and the use of VPNs help protect against such threats, but attackers continue to find ways to exploit weak encryption, expired certificates, or poorly configured systems.

Supply chain attacks have emerged as a significant and growing concern. These attacks occur when an adversary targets a trusted third party, such as a software vendor or service provider, in order to compromise its clients. By injecting malicious code into a legitimate software update or compromising a widely used platform, attackers can gain access to thousands of networks simultaneously. The infamous SolarWinds attack is a prime example, where a compromised update affected numerous government and private sector organizations. Supply chain threats highlight the importance of verifying the security practices of partners and suppliers and continuously monitoring for unusual behavior even from trusted sources.

Cloud environments also introduce unique security challenges. While cloud providers offer robust infrastructure, the shared responsibility model means that customers are responsible for securing their data, identities, and configurations. Misconfigured cloud storage, exposed APIs, and weak identity management can all lead to breaches. Attackers often exploit these weaknesses to gain unauthorized access to cloud resources, mine cryptocurrency, or steal data. As more organizations migrate to the cloud, ensuring proper configuration, visibility, and control becomes essential for maintaining security.

The proliferation of Internet of Things devices has further expanded the threat landscape. These devices often lack adequate security controls and may use default credentials or outdated firmware, making them easy targets for attackers. Once compromised, IoT devices can be used to spy on users, disrupt services, or serve as entry points into larger networks. Managing the security of IoT devices requires regular updates, segmentation, and continuous monitoring to detect anomalous behavior.

Threats in modern network environments are diverse, evolving, and increasingly difficult to detect and prevent. As technology advances and attackers develop new methods, staying ahead requires not only strong technical defenses but also a strategic and adaptive approach to security. This includes investing in threat intelligence, employing advanced monitoring tools, conducting regular risk assessments, and fostering a culture of security awareness throughout the organization. Only through a combination of vigilance, education, and innovation can networks remain resilient in the face of these ever-present and growing dangers.

Overview of Security Protocol Families

Security protocols form the backbone of secure communication and data protection in modern computing environments. They define the rules and procedures for protecting the confidentiality, integrity, and authenticity of data as it moves across networks or is stored in various systems. These protocols operate at different layers of the communication stack and are tailored to meet the diverse requirements of applications, services, and infrastructures. Security protocol families consist of collections of related protocols designed to work together to provide comprehensive protection. Understanding these protocol families is critical for ensuring the safe operation of systems and for defending against a broad spectrum of cyber threats.

One of the most well-known security protocol families is the Secure Sockets Layer and its successor, the Transport Layer Security protocol. These protocols operate between the transport and application layers of the OSI model, enabling encrypted communication between clients and servers. TLS is widely used to secure web traffic, email, messaging services, and voice-over-IP. When a user accesses a secure website via HTTPS, TLS is responsible for establishing a secure session through a process known as the handshake. During the handshake, both parties exchange cryptographic information, authenticate each other using digital certificates, and agree upon a shared session key for encrypting subsequent communication. TLS also ensures message integrity through the use of message authentication codes. The TLS protocol family has evolved through several versions, each addressing vulnerabilities and improving cryptographic strength. Modern implementations of TLS have deprecated older, insecure features such as SSLv3 and weak cipher suites to keep pace with emerging threats and computational advances.

Another critical security protocol family is IPsec, or Internet Protocol Security. IPsec operates at the network layer and is used to secure IP communications by authenticating and encrypting each IP packet in a communication session. Unlike TLS, which protects individual applications, IPsec can be applied more broadly to secure all data passing between two endpoints at the network layer. It is commonly used in virtual private networks, enabling secure communication between remote users and corporate networks over public internet connections. IPsec protocols include the Authentication Header, which ensures the integrity and authenticity of packets, and the Encapsulating Security Payload, which provides encryption for confidentiality. These protocols work in conjunction with Internet Key Exchange, which manages the negotiation and setup of security associations and cryptographic keys. IPsec supports both transport mode, where only the payload is encrypted, and tunnel mode, where the entire packet is protected. This flexibility makes it suitable for securing end-to-end communication as well as network-to-network connections.

The Kerberos protocol family is another major component of enterprise-level security. Kerberos is a network authentication protocol designed to provide secure authentication for users and services in a distributed environment. It is widely implemented in corporate networks and integrated with directory services such as Active Directory. The protocol uses a trusted third-party system, known as a Key Distribution Center, to issue time-limited tickets that grant access to services. By relying on shared secrets and encrypted tickets, Kerberos eliminates the need to transmit passwords over the network. It also protects against replay attacks and impersonation through the use of timestamps and mutual authentication. Kerberos is particularly effective in environments with multiple interconnected services that require a centralized authentication mechanism. Its ability to authenticate users without exposing credentials directly contributes significantly to the security of enterprise infrastructure.

The Secure Shell protocol family is essential for secure remote administration and file transfers. SSH provides a secure channel over an insecure network by using public-key cryptography for authentication and symmetric encryption for confidentiality. SSH replaces older protocols like Telnet and FTP, which transmitted credentials in plaintext, making them highly vulnerable to interception. SSH includes multiple components such as SCP for secure file copying, SFTP for secure file transfer, and port forwarding to enable encrypted tunnels for other applications. The strength of SSH lies in its combination of security features, including strong encryption, integrity checking, and support for various authentication methods such as passwords, public keys, and certificates. SSH is widely used by system administrators to manage servers, configure network devices, and automate scripts, making it an indispensable tool for secure network operations.

The Simple Network Management Protocol also has a family of security enhancements that ensure secure monitoring and management of networked devices. SNMP is used to collect and organize information about devices on IP networks and to modify that information to change device behavior. While earlier versions of SNMP had limited or no security features, SNMPv3 introduced significant improvements, including support for authentication, message integrity, and encryption. These enhancements ensure that network management data cannot be tampered with or viewed by unauthorized parties. In environments where network infrastructure is remotely managed or frequently updated, the use of secure SNMP protocols is critical for maintaining operational integrity and preventing malicious interference.

Wireless communication protocols also fall under security protocol families. The IEEE 802.11 standards for Wi-Fi include protocols such as WPA2 and WPA3, which secure wireless networks through authentication and encryption mechanisms. WPA2 uses the AES encryption algorithm and includes features like the four-way handshake to establish a shared key between the client and the access point. WPA3 builds on this by introducing stronger encryption, improved key exchange through Simultaneous Authentication of Equals, and protections against offline dictionary attacks. These protocols are essential for protecting wireless networks from unauthorized access, data interception, and manipulation, especially in environments where sensitive information is transmitted over Wi-Fi.

Another important family is the authentication, authorization, and accounting protocols used in access control systems. Protocols such as RADIUS and TACACS+ enable centralized authentication of users who access network resources. These protocols ensure that users are properly identified, granted appropriate permissions, and that their activity is logged for auditing purposes. RADIUS is commonly used in conjunction with Wi-Fi authentication, VPNs, and network infrastructure devices, while TACACS+ offers more granular control and separation of authentication and authorization processes. By implementing these protocols, organizations can manage user access efficiently and ensure accountability in system usage.

Security protocol families play a critical role in maintaining trust in digital systems. Each family addresses specific aspects of communication and protection, whether it is securing data in transit, verifying user identities, controlling access to resources, or protecting against eavesdropping and tampering. The overlapping nature of these protocols allows them to be combined into layered defenses that address a wide range of attack vectors. As cyber threats evolve and new vulnerabilities are discovered, the continued development and refinement of security protocols are essential for preserving the confidentiality, integrity, and availability of information systems. Understanding how these protocol families function and interact is a foundational skill for cybersecurity professionals and a key component of designing secure architectures in an increasingly connected world.

IPsec: An Introduction

IPsec, short for Internet Protocol Security, is a suite of protocols designed to secure communications over IP networks by providing confidentiality, integrity, and authentication at the network layer. It is one of the most powerful and flexible security tools available, enabling secure point-to-point or site-to-site connections over both private and public networks. What sets IPsec apart is its deep integration with the IP layer itself, meaning it can protect all traffic regardless of the application or protocol in use. This broad protection makes it a key component in the construction of virtual private networks and in securing data that traverses untrusted networks such as the internet.

Operating at the network layer allows IPsec to function independently of application protocols. Unlike TLS, which must be implemented at the application level and configured per service, IPsec works transparently to applications. This means that once an IPsec tunnel is established between two endpoints, any application on those endpoints can benefit from encrypted and authenticated communication without requiring modification. IPsec is also scalable, capable of securing communication between individual hosts, networks, or even entire enterprises.

IPsec functions using a combination of protocols and cryptographic techniques. The two main components of IPsec are the Authentication Header and the Encapsulating Security Payload. The Authentication Header provides connectionless integrity and data origin authentication for IP packets. It ensures that the data has not been tampered with in transit and verifies the identity of the sender. However, it does not provide encryption. For scenarios where confidentiality is also needed, the Encapsulating Security Payload is used. ESP provides encryption of the packet payload, as well as optional integrity and authentication. ESP can be used alone or in combination with the Authentication Header, depending on the security needs of the network environment.

To establish secure connections, IPsec uses a process known as Security Association negotiation. This process determines how two devices will communicate securely, including what algorithms and keys will be used. Security Associations are one-way logical connections that define the parameters of a secure communication session. Every IPsec connection involves at least two Security Associations, one for each direction of communication. These associations include information such as encryption and authentication algorithms, keys, and the lifetime of the connection.

Managing Security Associations and cryptographic keys is handled by a protocol called the Internet Key Exchange. IKE plays a critical role in the establishment and maintenance of IPsec connections. It negotiates the parameters of the Security Associations and handles the secure exchange of keys using techniques such as the Diffie-Hellman key exchange. IKE operates in two phases. In the first phase, a secure channel is established between the two parties, called the IKE Security Association. In the second phase, this secure channel is used to negotiate the actual IPsec Security Associations that will protect the IP traffic. Modern implementations of IPsec use IKE version 2, which improves upon the original IKE by providing better performance, enhanced security, and support for mobility and multihoming.

IPsec can operate in two different modes: transport mode and tunnel mode. Transport mode is used to secure end-to-end communication between two hosts. In this mode, only the payload of the IP packet is encrypted or authenticated, while the original IP header remains intact. This allows routers to forward the packet normally, which is useful when both endpoints are within the same trusted network. Tunnel mode, on the other hand, is used for network-to-network or host-to-network communication. In tunnel mode, the entire original IP packet is encrypted and encapsulated within a new packet with a new IP header. This mode is commonly used in VPNs to connect remote offices or users to a central network securely over the internet.

IPsec is particularly popular in enterprise environments for building secure VPNs. Organizations use IPsec to ensure that remote workers can access internal resources as if they were physically present in the office, without exposing sensitive data to the public internet. It is also used to connect branch offices, datacenters, and cloud environments in a secure manner. Because IPsec is supported by most major operating systems, network equipment, and firewalls, it offers a standardized and interoperable method for building secure communications across diverse infrastructure.

Despite its advantages, IPsec is not without challenges. One of the complexities lies in its configuration. Setting up IPsec correctly requires detailed knowledge of encryption algorithms, key lifetimes, and policy settings. Misconfigurations can lead to degraded security or even prevent communication altogether. Furthermore, because IPsec encrypts at the network layer, it can interfere with certain network diagnostic tools and performance monitoring, which rely on examining packet contents or headers. Network address translation can also pose issues for IPsec, particularly in transport mode, since NAT modifies IP headers that are often used in IPsec authentication.

To address these challenges, many implementations of IPsec include features designed to simplify configuration and improve compatibility. For instance, NAT Traversal allows IPsec packets to be encapsulated in UDP packets, enabling them to pass through NAT devices more reliably. Modern VPN gateways often provide graphical interfaces or automated setup wizards to reduce the complexity of deploying IPsec tunnels. Additionally, standardization efforts ensure that different vendors' IPsec implementations can interoperate, which is vital in multi-vendor environments.

IPsec continues to evolve to meet the needs of changing network architectures. With the rise of cloud computing and hybrid infrastructures, organizations increasingly need secure and flexible connections between on-premises networks and cloud providers. IPsec is frequently used to establish site-to-site VPNs that connect private datacenters to cloud environments, enabling secure data exchange and extending internal network policies to remote systems. In mobile environments, IPsec's ability to support mobility and dynamic IP addresses, especially with IKEv2, ensures that users remain protected even as they move between networks or change locations.

Security protocols like IPsec are vital in defending against modern cyber threats. By securing data at the network layer, IPsec shields sensitive traffic from interception, manipulation, and unauthorized access. It plays an essential role in regulatory compliance for data protection and is a trusted solution for building robust, secure communications. As organizations continue to face growing security demands and increasingly complex network landscapes, the role of IPsec remains critical in enabling safe, encrypted, and authenticated communication across distributed systems.

IPsec Architecture and Components

IPsec, or Internet Protocol Security, is a comprehensive framework designed to secure communication over IP networks through encryption, authentication, and integrity verification. It operates primarily at the network layer of the OSI model and provides security features that protect IP packets traveling between hosts, gateways, or networks. Understanding the architecture of IPsec is essential for grasping how it achieves its security objectives. The architecture includes a set of protocols, components, and operational modes that work together to provide confidentiality, data integrity, origin authentication, and protection against replay attacks.

At the core of IPsec architecture is the concept of Security Associations. A Security Association is a one-way logical connection that provides the parameters required for secure communication, such as the encryption algorithm, the authentication method, the keys used, and the lifetime of the session. For bidirectional communication, two Security Associations are needed—one for each direction. These associations are identified by a unique Security Parameter Index, combined with the destination IP address and the security protocol in use. Each SA defines how traffic is protected and ensures that the communicating parties are aligned on the methods being applied.

To create and manage Security Associations, IPsec relies on the Internet Key Exchange protocol. IKE is responsible for negotiating and establishing SAs between peers, exchanging cryptographic keys securely, and verifying identities. IKE functions in two phases. During Phase 1, a secure channel known as the IKE SA is established using asymmetric cryptographic methods and Diffie-Hellman key exchange. This phase provides a secure foundation for further negotiation. In Phase 2, the peers use this secure channel to negotiate one or more IPsec SAs that will protect actual user data. IKEv2, the current version of the protocol, introduced significant improvements in efficiency, support for mobility, and resistance to denial-of-service attacks. It also simplified the message structure and added better error handling compared to its predecessor.

Within the IPsec protocol suite, two main protocols carry out the core functions of data protection: the Authentication Header and the Encapsulating Security Payload. The Authentication Header provides integrity and origin authentication for IP packets. It ensures that the packet has not been altered in transit and that it was sent by a verified source. However, it does not encrypt the payload, which means confidentiality is not provided. The Encapsulating Security Payload, on the other hand, offers both encryption and optional authentication. ESP is capable of providing confidentiality, integrity, and origin authentication, making it the more commonly used of the two. ESP can encrypt the payload and other parts of the IP packet, depending on the mode of operation selected.

IPsec can function in two operational modes: transport mode and tunnel mode. In transport mode, only the payload of the IP packet is encrypted or authenticated, while the original IP header is left intact. This mode is typically used for end-to-end communication between two hosts. It allows routers to forward the packet normally since the header is visible, but the data is still protected. In tunnel mode, the entire original IP packet is encrypted and encapsulated within a new IP packet with a new header. This creates a secure tunnel between two IPsec peers, such as gateways or firewalls, and is commonly used for site-to-site virtual private networks. Tunnel mode hides both the payload and the original header, which enhances security but requires that the encapsulating devices be capable of routing based on the new outer headers.

Another fundamental element of the IPsec architecture is the Security Policy Database. The SPD is a set of rules that determine how and when IPsec should be applied to outbound or inbound traffic. Each entry in the SPD specifies a traffic selector, such as source and destination IP addresses or ports, and the corresponding action to take. The actions can include discarding the traffic, bypassing IPsec, or protecting it with IPsec. When a packet is processed, the SPD is consulted to determine the appropriate handling. If protection is required, the Security Association Database is queried to locate an appropriate SA, or a new SA is negotiated through IKE if none exists.

IPsec implementations also incorporate anti-replay protection. Replay attacks occur when an attacker captures legitimate packets and retransmits them in an attempt to deceive the receiving system. To prevent this, IPsec maintains a sliding window of sequence numbers for each SA. Packets received with a duplicate or out-of-sequence number outside the current window are rejected. This mechanism ensures that each packet is unique and has not been tampered with or resent by a malicious actor.

Authentication in IPsec can be achieved using pre-shared keys, digital certificates, or public key infrastructure. Pre-shared keys are simple to implement but are less scalable and secure in large environments. Digital certificates, issued by trusted certificate authorities, provide a higher level of trust and scalability. IPsec uses these methods to verify the identity of peers during IKE negotiation, ensuring that only authorized devices can participate in secure communication.

Certificate-based authentication also supports more granular access control and is often used in enterprise and government networks.

The architecture of IPsec allows for both host-based and gateway-based deployments. In host-based IPsec, the protocol is implemented on the individual endpoint devices, such as laptops or servers. This provides granular control over which traffic is secured and is ideal for remote access scenarios. In gateway-based IPsec, security is managed by dedicated devices like firewalls or VPN concentrators. These devices establish tunnels on behalf of internal hosts and are commonly used to connect entire networks. This centralizes security management and simplifies the enforcement of security policies.

IPsec is supported by most modern operating systems, including Windows, Linux, macOS, and various flavors of Unix. It is also widely implemented in enterprise-grade networking hardware. Its flexibility, strong security guarantees, and standards-based approach make it a preferred solution for securing data at the IP layer. Whether protecting communication between datacenters, enabling secure remote access, or connecting branch offices over untrusted networks, IPsec provides a robust and scalable architecture for network security. Its modular design and comprehensive set of components allow organizations to tailor deployments according to specific needs, making it a cornerstone of modern secure networking practices.

Internet Key Exchange (IKE and IKEv2)

The Internet Key Exchange protocol, commonly referred to as IKE, is a cornerstone of the IPsec suite and serves the essential function of establishing secure communication channels between two parties over an IP network. It is responsible for negotiating, creating, and managing Security Associations, which are the foundational agreements used in IPsec to define the parameters for encrypting and authenticating data. Without a mechanism like IKE, the process of securely exchanging cryptographic keys would be vulnerable to interception and manipulation by unauthorized entities. The development of IKE represented a significant advancement in secure networking, as it enabled dynamic, scalable, and automated configuration of secure connections without requiring manual key distribution.

IKE operates by combining several protocols and techniques. It draws on the principles of the Internet Security Association and Key Management Protocol, or ISAKMP, to define how peers communicate, negotiate policies, and manage the lifecycle of Security Associations. It also uses elements of the Oakley Key Determination Protocol to provide a secure method of key exchange using the Diffie-Hellman algorithm. Diffie-Hellman enables two parties to generate a shared secret over an insecure channel, which is fundamental to the cryptographic strength of IKE. The integration of these components allows IKE to perform mutual authentication, select security protocols and algorithms, and generate the cryptographic keys required for secure communication.

The original version of IKE, now referred to as IKEv1, operates in two distinct phases. In Phase 1, the two peers establish a secure, authenticated communication channel known as the IKE Security Association. This channel is protected using encryption and authentication methods agreed upon by both parties. During this phase, the peers also authenticate each other using pre-shared keys, digital certificates, or public key encryption. Once the secure channel is established, Phase 2 begins. In this phase, the peers use the secure IKE channel to negotiate one or more IPsec Security Associations, which will be used to protect actual IP traffic. Each SA includes details such as the encryption algorithm, hash function, and lifetime of the connection. These associations define how the data will be encrypted, authenticated, and validated for the duration of the session.

While IKEv1 provided a functional and secure key exchange mechanism, it had several limitations that became more apparent as network environments grew more complex. The protocol was relatively complex and difficult to implement consistently across platforms. It also lacked native support for features like NAT traversal and mobility, which became increasingly important in modern networking. Additionally, IKEv1 had ambiguous behaviors in some scenarios, leading to interoperability issues and making troubleshooting difficult. These challenges led to the development of an improved version of the protocol, known as IKEv2.

IKEv2 was designed to address the shortcomings of its predecessor while maintaining the core functionality and security guarantees. It simplifies the negotiation process by reducing the number of messages exchanged and clarifying the protocol's behavior. IKEv2 combines the two-phase structure of IKEv1 into a more streamlined exchange. The initial exchange of messages performs both authentication and key agreement, allowing the peers to establish the IKE SA and the first IPsec SA in a single process. This efficiency reduces the time and resources required to set up a secure session and makes the protocol more resilient to network delays and packet loss.

One of the most notable features of IKEv2 is its support for Mobility and Multihoming through the MOBIKE extension. This capability allows devices to maintain secure connections even as they change IP addresses or network interfaces, which is critical in mobile environments. For example, a user moving between Wi-Fi and cellular networks can maintain a persistent VPN connection without needing to renegotiate a new session. This is particularly important for modern devices that rely on continuous connectivity, such as smartphones, tablets, and laptops used by remote workers.

IKEv2 also includes built-in support for Network Address Translation traversal. Many network environments use NAT to conserve IP addresses, which can interfere with the proper functioning of security protocols like IPsec. IKEv2 detects when NAT is present and automatically adjusts the communication process to encapsulate IPsec packets in UDP, ensuring that they can traverse NAT devices without being blocked or altered. This feature greatly enhances the compatibility of IPsec across diverse network topologies and is a significant improvement over the limited and inconsistent NAT traversal mechanisms of IKEv1.

Security in IKEv2 is further enhanced through its use of modern cryptographic algorithms and its robust error handling mechanisms. The protocol supports a wide range of encryption and authentication methods, including AES, SHA-2, and elliptic curve cryptography, allowing it to meet stringent security requirements. Its modular design makes it easy to add support for new algorithms as cryptographic standards evolve. Furthermore, IKEv2 provides clear and consistent error messages, enabling better diagnostics and more straightforward debugging when issues arise.

Another key improvement in IKEv2 is its resistance to denial-of-service attacks. The protocol uses a mechanism called cookie challenges to verify the legitimacy of connection requests before allocating significant resources to a session. When a new request is received, the responder can issue a cookie challenge that the initiator must return before the exchange proceeds. This prevents attackers from overwhelming a device with fake requests, helping to maintain the stability and availability of the network.

IKEv2's state machine is also more predictable and easier to manage than that of IKEv1. This makes the protocol not only easier to implement but also more secure, as there are fewer ambiguous states or transitions that could be exploited by attackers. The protocol is also designed with extensibility in mind, allowing new features and capabilities to be added without disrupting existing functionality. This forward-looking design ensures that IKEv2 can adapt to future networking challenges and technological developments.

Today, IKEv2 is widely supported across platforms and devices, including Windows, Linux, macOS, iOS, and Android. It is the preferred method for establishing secure IPsec VPN connections in many enterprise environments due to its efficiency, flexibility, and strong security posture. Its ability to operate smoothly across different types of networks and to support modern use cases such as mobile connectivity and cloud integration makes it an indispensable part of the secure internet infrastructure.

The Internet Key Exchange protocol, in both its original and updated forms, represents a critical advancement in the field of secure communication. It enables the dynamic and secure exchange of cryptographic keys, ensures that only authorized devices can establish protected channels, and provides the foundation upon which the broader IPsec framework operates. As digital communication continues to expand and evolve, the role of protocols like IKE and IKEv2 remains essential in safeguarding the data that flows through global networks.

IPsec Modes: Transport and Tunnel

IPsec, or Internet Protocol Security, is a powerful suite of protocols used to secure IP communications by authenticating and encrypting each IP packet in a given communication session. It operates at the network layer and provides a set of standards for securing data as it travels across untrusted networks. A fundamental aspect of IPsec is its ability to operate in two distinct modes: transport mode and tunnel mode. Each of these modes serves a specific purpose and is suitable for different types of network configurations and use cases. Understanding how transport and tunnel modes function is essential for effectively deploying IPsec in a variety of network security architectures.

Transport mode is primarily used for securing end-to-end communications between two hosts. In this mode, only the payload of the IP packet is encrypted and/or authenticated, while the original IP header is left intact. This allows intermediate devices such as routers and switches to process and forward the packet based on its destination address. Transport mode is ideal for scenarios where the devices at both ends of the communication are directly participating in the IPsec session, such as two servers exchanging sensitive information or a user device communicating securely with a specific application server.

Because the original IP header remains unchanged in transport mode, the integrity of the network routing process is preserved. Devices along the path can inspect the packet headers and make routing decisions without the need to decrypt any portion of the data. This mode provides confidentiality through encryption of the payload, data integrity through cryptographic hash functions, and origin authentication by verifying the identity of the sender. Although the header remains exposed, the protection of the payload is often sufficient in environments where the internal network is already considered secure or where performance is a critical concern.

However, the exposure of the IP header in transport mode also presents limitations. Because the header is not encrypted, an attacker with access to the network can still see information such as the source and destination IP addresses, which could be used for traffic analysis or mapping network topologies. For this reason, transport mode is generally used within trusted environments or for specific communications where full packet encapsulation is not necessary. It is also worth noting that transport mode is often used in combination with other security mechanisms, such as application-layer encryption or secure tunneling protocols, to achieve layered defense.

Tunnel mode, on the other hand, is designed for securing communications between networks or between a host and a network. In tunnel mode, the entire original IP packet—including both the header and the payload—is encrypted and then encapsulated within a new IP packet that has a new IP header. This new header allows the encapsulated packet to be routed through intermediate networks without revealing the details of the original packet. Tunnel mode is typically used for site-to-site virtual private networks, where two gateways establish a secure tunnel to connect different parts of a distributed network over the internet or other untrusted infrastructure.

By encrypting the entire original packet, tunnel mode offers a higher level of security and anonymity. Not only is the payload protected from interception, but the identities of the communicating parties are also concealed from external observers. This makes tunnel mode the preferred choice for organizations seeking to connect branch offices, datacenters, or remote users to central corporate networks. The encrypted tunnel acts as a secure conduit through which all traffic flows, and the endpoints at either side of the tunnel are responsible for encrypting and decrypting the traffic as it enters and leaves the secure channel.

Tunnel mode also facilitates network address translation and hiding, as internal IP addresses are not visible beyond the tunnel endpoint. This helps prevent external attackers from identifying internal network structures and devices, thereby reducing the potential attack surface. Furthermore, tunnel mode is compatible with a wide range of IPsec implementations and can be used in conjunction with other security technologies such as firewalls, intrusion detection systems, and access control mechanisms to create a comprehensive and resilient security posture.

One of the most common use cases for tunnel mode is the creation of remote-access VPNs. In this configuration, a remote user connects to a corporate VPN gateway over the internet. The VPN client on the user's device encapsulates and encrypts the traffic, which is then sent through the IPsec tunnel to the gateway. Once decrypted, the traffic is forwarded into the internal network as if the user were physically present on the premises. This enables secure access to internal resources such as file servers, databases, and enterprise applications from virtually any location, while maintaining strict control over data confidentiality and integrity.

The implementation of either transport or tunnel mode is determined by the specific needs of the network environment. For example, in a host-to-host scenario where performance is a priority and the network is already protected by other means, transport mode may be the preferred option. In contrast, for communications across public networks or between different segments of a corporate network, tunnel mode provides stronger security and better traffic encapsulation. Both modes rely on the same underlying IPsec protocols, including the Authentication Header and the Encapsulating Security Payload, to provide their security services. The choice of mode affects how these protocols are applied and how the resulting packets are structured and processed.

From a technical perspective, the main difference between the two modes lies in the placement and construction of headers during the encapsulation process. In transport mode, the IP header is followed directly by the IPsec header and then the protected payload. In tunnel mode, the IPsec header is inserted before a completely new IP packet that includes both a new header and the original, now encrypted, packet. This structural difference is crucial when designing IPsec policies and configuring devices to handle secure traffic appropriately.

Interoperability and policy enforcement are also key considerations when choosing between transport and tunnel modes. Devices and systems involved in the communication must support the chosen mode and be properly configured to apply the corresponding security policies. Misconfiguration can result in traffic being dropped, delays in establishing secure connections, or vulnerabilities that could be exploited by attackers. Careful planning, testing, and documentation are essential to ensure that IPsec deployments using either transport or tunnel mode achieve the intended security objectives.

IPsec's flexibility in supporting these two modes of operation is one of its greatest strengths. It allows network architects to tailor security solutions to a wide variety of use cases, balancing the trade-offs between performance, visibility, and confidentiality. Whether protecting a single data stream between two servers or securing an entire enterprise's communications over a public network, the proper use of transport and tunnel modes enables organizations to confidently exchange data in an increasingly hostile digital environment. Through careful configuration and ongoing monitoring, IPsec in both modes can be a powerful tool for maintaining secure, trusted communication across today's diverse network infrastructures.

IPsec Authentication Header (AH)

The Authentication Header, commonly known as AH, is one of the two primary protocols within the IPsec suite. While the Encapsulating Security Payload focuses on providing confidentiality through encryption, the Authentication Header serves a different yet equally vital role in securing network communications. It is designed to provide connectionless integrity, data origin authentication, and optional anti-replay protection for IP packets. By ensuring that data has not been altered in transit and verifying the identity of the sender, AH enhances trust in communication between devices over untrusted networks. Though AH does not offer encryption and thus does not hide the contents of the data, its ability to detect unauthorized modifications makes it a critical component in scenarios where integrity and authenticity are paramount.

AH operates by adding an additional header to each IP packet. This header contains a cryptographic checksum, known as the Integrity Check Value, which is calculated using a hash function and a shared secret key. When a packet is received, the recipient recalculates the checksum and compares it to the one included in the AH. If they match, the packet is assumed to have arrived without alteration and from a verified source. If the values differ, the packet is rejected. This process allows AH to protect against many common network attacks, including tampering, spoofing, and replay attacks, especially when combined with proper sequence number management.

The position of the Authentication Header within the packet structure depends on the mode in which IPsec is operating. In transport mode, AH is inserted between the original IP header and the payload. This placement allows the protocol to authenticate the entire IP packet except for fields that change in transit, such as the Time to Live or checksum fields. In tunnel mode, the entire original IP packet, including its header, is encapsulated and treated as the payload of a new packet, and the AH is applied to the encapsulating header. This means that in tunnel mode, AH can authenticate not only the payload but also the original IP header, offering a more comprehensive protection of the data and its source.

One of the defining characteristics of AH is that it protects the immutable parts of the IP header along with the packet's payload. Immutable fields are those that are not expected to change as the packet traverses the network. This includes source and destination IP addresses, protocol identifier, and other fixed header fields. By including these fields in the integrity check, AH ensures that a packet has not been redirected or altered in a way that could compromise the security or reliability of the communication. This level of protection is especially important in environments where header manipulation could be used to bypass security policies or reroute traffic maliciously.

Despite its strengths, AH also comes with some limitations that have led to its reduced use in favor of the Encapsulating Security Payload in many modern implementations. Since AH does not encrypt any part of the packet, all content remains visible to anyone who intercepts the traffic. This exposure may be unacceptable in scenarios where confidentiality is required. Additionally, AH's coverage of parts of the IP header creates compatibility issues with network address translation devices, which modify IP headers in transit. Because AH includes the IP addresses in its integrity check, even legitimate NAT operations will cause the hash to fail, resulting in rejected packets. This makes AH difficult to deploy in environments that use NAT, which are common in both enterprise and consumer networks.

Despite these limitations, AH remains valuable in specific use cases. In highly controlled network environments where NAT is not present and where transparency of packet contents is desirable or required for regulatory or operational reasons, AH provides an effective way to ensure the authenticity and integrity of communication. It is also useful in conjunction with systems that perform detailed packet inspection or logging, where encrypted payloads would hinder visibility. In such cases, using AH allows network administrators to monitor traffic while still verifying its legitimacy.

From a technical perspective, the integrity check used by AH is based on cryptographic hash functions such as HMAC combined with SHA-1, SHA-2, or other algorithms depending on the security requirements and the implementation. The shared key used to generate the hash is agreed upon during the Internet Key Exchange process and stored within the Security Association that governs the IPsec session. AH also includes a sequence number field that helps defend against replay attacks by allowing the receiver to detect and reject duplicate packets. This mechanism requires maintaining a sliding window of acceptable sequence numbers and comparing each incoming packet to determine whether it is new, valid, or suspiciously repeated.

Implementation of AH requires careful coordination between endpoints to ensure proper alignment of policies, keys, and expected behaviors. Devices must agree on which traffic will be protected by AH, what algorithms will be used, and how sequence numbers will be handled. The Security Policy Database and Security Association Database within the IPsec architecture manage these configurations and ensure that packets are processed according to defined rules. Misconfiguration can result in rejected traffic, reduced performance, or exposure to attack, highlighting the importance of thorough planning and testing when deploying AH.

AH can be used alone or in combination with ESP, depending on the security needs of the network. In some deployments, AH is applied to provide integrity and authentication, while ESP is used to encrypt the payload, combining the strengths of both protocols. This dual use allows for flexible and robust security policies that address a wide range of threats. However, as modern security needs increasingly require both confidentiality and integrity, ESP has become the default choice in most IPsec configurations, often with its own authentication mechanisms included, which reduces the need for AH as a standalone solution.

Nevertheless, AH continues to be supported by major IPsec implementations and remains part of the standardized framework defined by the Internet Engineering Task Force. Its presence in the protocol suite provides security architects with an additional tool for designing tailored solutions, especially in specialized scenarios where its unique features are advantageous. Understanding how AH works, what it protects, and where it fits into the broader IPsec framework is essential for anyone responsible for securing IP communications. By focusing on data integrity and authentication, AH contributes to the overall trustworthiness of network interactions, ensuring that data arrives intact and from a verified source in an increasingly complex and hostile digital landscape.

IPsec Encapsulating Security Payload (ESP)

The Encapsulating Security Payload, or ESP, is one of the two core protocols of the IPsec suite, designed to provide confidentiality, integrity, and authentication for IP packets transmitted across potentially insecure networks. ESP is a critical tool in protecting the data that flows through public and private infrastructures alike. It allows organizations to ensure that their sensitive communications remain hidden from unauthorized observers, tamper-proof during transmission, and verifiably authentic. Unlike its counterpart, the Authentication Header, which only provides integrity and authentication, ESP also includes robust encryption capabilities, making it the more commonly used of the two in modern secure networking deployments.

ESP works by encapsulating the original data payload of an IP packet within a secure wrapper that encrypts the data and optionally authenticates the entire package. This encapsulation process ensures that even if a packet is intercepted during its journey across the network, its contents remain unreadable to anyone who does not possess the appropriate cryptographic keys. In addition to protecting the data itself, ESP can also provide verification that the data has not been altered in transit and that it was indeed sent by the claimed source, assuming integrity and authentication services are enabled.

ESP can operate in two modes: transport mode and tunnel mode. In transport mode, ESP protects the payload of the IP packet, leaving the original IP header intact. This mode is generally used in host-to-host communications where both endpoints are directly involved in the encryption and decryption processes. It allows for efficient data protection while still enabling intermediate routers and devices to examine the IP header for routing purposes. In tunnel mode, ESP encrypts and encapsulates the entire original IP packet, including its header. The encrypted packet is then wrapped inside a new IP packet with a fresh header that contains routing information. Tunnel mode is typically used for gateway-to-gateway or host-to-gateway scenarios, such as Virtual Private Network implementations, where a secure tunnel is created between two endpoints to protect all the traffic passing between them.

The structure of an ESP packet includes several components. At the beginning of the ESP section is the Security Parameters Index, a unique identifier that tells the receiving system which Security Association to use for processing the packet. This is followed by a sequence number, which helps protect against replay attacks by ensuring that packets are not duplicated or reordered without detection. The encrypted portion of the packet includes the original data payload, padding (if needed for block-aligned encryption), and the next header field, which identifies the type of protocol encapsulated within ESP. Finally, if integrity and authentication are enabled, an Integrity Check Value is appended to the packet, calculated using a cryptographic hash function to ensure that the data has not been altered.

The encryption algorithms used by ESP can vary depending on the specific configuration and the cryptographic policies agreed upon during the Internet Key Exchange process. Common choices include the Advanced Encryption Standard, or AES, which is widely used due to its strength and efficiency. ESP supports a variety of encryption modes, such as Cipher Block Chaining and Galois/Counter Mode, each offering different balances of performance and security. The use of modern, well-tested algorithms ensures that ESP provides strong confidentiality guarantees against brute-force and cryptanalytic attacks.

When integrity and authentication are desired, ESP uses Hash-based Message Authentication Codes, such as HMAC with SHA-256, to produce the Integrity Check Value. This value allows the recipient to verify that the packet has not been tampered with and that it comes from a trusted source. While these features are optional in ESP, they are commonly used in secure configurations to provide complete protection against a wide range of network threats. In fact, in many implementations, both encryption and integrity are enabled by default, reflecting best practices in secure communications.

ESP is designed to be flexible and extensible, accommodating a wide range of deployment scenarios. It supports both IPv4 and IPv6 and is compatible with various network topologies and devices. Because ESP encrypts the data, it also helps reduce the risk of information leakage through traffic analysis, where an attacker attempts to glean information from patterns in unencrypted data flows. By obscuring the contents and structure of the communication, ESP makes such analysis significantly more difficult.

One of the challenges associated with ESP, particularly in transport mode, is compatibility with devices that perform Network Address Translation. Since NAT modifies the IP header and ESP does not include ports or session-level identifiers in its encapsulation, some configurations can lead to issues in traversal. To address this, IPsec implementations often use NAT Traversal, which encapsulates ESP packets inside UDP packets, allowing them to pass through NAT devices more effectively. This feature has become an essential part of ESP deployments in modern networks, especially in mobile and cloud-based environments.

ESP is widely supported across operating systems, network hardware, and security appliances. Its integration into VPN solutions allows organizations to securely connect remote sites, mobile users, and cloud resources, while preserving the confidentiality and integrity of sensitive data. From securing emails and file transfers to enabling protected voice and video communication, ESP forms a foundational layer in countless secure communications systems around the world.

Administrators configuring ESP must pay close attention to cryptographic strength, key management, and policy enforcement. The strength of the encryption and hashing algorithms directly impacts the level of security provided, while key negotiation protocols such as IKE ensure that keys are exchanged securely and regularly refreshed. Security policies defined in the Security Policy Database determine which traffic should be protected by ESP and how it should be processed. Proper configuration and maintenance of these components are essential to avoid misconfigurations that could undermine security.

As cyber threats continue to evolve, the role of ESP in safeguarding digital communications remains vital. It provides a reliable and standards-based method for protecting data at the network layer, ensuring that even if attackers intercept traffic, they cannot read or manipulate the information. With its combination of confidentiality, authentication, and flexibility, ESP remains the preferred mechanism for securing IP packets in a wide range of network environments. Its continued development and adoption underscore the importance of strong encryption and data integrity in maintaining the trust and resilience of global communication networks.

IPsec Policy Configuration and Management

IPsec policy configuration and management play a critical role in ensuring that the security services provided by IPsec are applied effectively and consistently across a network. The strength and reliability of an IPsec deployment depend not only on the underlying cryptographic protocols but also on how policies are defined, implemented, and maintained. These policies dictate how data traffic should be protected, which endpoints can communicate securely, what cryptographic algorithms should be used, and how keys are exchanged and managed. Proper policy configuration ensures that sensitive information remains protected while maintaining the usability and performance of the network.

At the heart of IPsec policy configuration are two fundamental data structures: the Security Policy Database (SPD) and the Security Association Database (SAD). The SPD contains a list of rules that determine how to handle packets entering or leaving a network interface. These rules include criteria for matching packets based on source and destination IP addresses, ports, and protocols, as well as the required actions, such as discarding the packet, allowing it through without protection, or applying IPsec security services. Each rule in the SPD reflects a policy decision made by the administrator and serves as a blueprint for handling different types of network traffic. When a packet matches a policy that calls for IPsec protection, the SPD ensures that the appropriate Security Association from the SAD is used to process it.

The SAD stores the parameters of each active Security Association, including the cryptographic algorithms, keys, lifetimes, and other attributes necessary to apply security to the packet. These SAs are unidirectional, meaning that separate SAs are required for traffic in each direction. When a policy requires protection but no matching SA exists, the system must negotiate a new one, typically using the Internet Key Exchange protocol. Once established, the SA allows packets to be processed according to the agreed-upon security mechanisms. This dynamic interaction between the SPD and SAD forms the core of IPsec's enforcement mechanism.

Policy configuration begins with identifying which traffic should be protected. This requires a clear understanding of the network's architecture, the data flows within it, and the security requirements of various applications and users. For example, traffic between branch offices might require full encryption and authentication, while internal traffic within a data center may only require integrity checks. Administrators must define policies that reflect these needs while avoiding overly broad rules that could unnecessarily burden the network or compromise performance. Proper segmentation of policies ensures that sensitive traffic receives appropriate protection while routine operations continue without disruption.

An effective IPsec policy must also specify the cryptographic algorithms to be used. These include encryption algorithms such as AES or ChaCha20, authentication algorithms such as HMAC-SHA2, and key exchange mechanisms such as Diffie-Hellman groups. The selection of these algorithms impacts both the security and performance of the system. Stronger algorithms provide better protection but may require more processing power, which could affect latency and throughput. Administrators must strike a balance between security and efficiency, often guided by organizational security standards or regulatory requirements.

Policy management also involves defining key lifetimes and rekeying intervals. Cryptographic keys should be changed regularly to limit the amount of data encrypted with a single key, thereby reducing the impact of a compromised key. Policies must define how long each SA remains valid and when it should be renegotiated. This process, known as rekeying, is handled automatically by IKE, but the timing and parameters are set by the administrator. Setting key lifetimes that are too short may cause frequent rekeying and unnecessary overhead, while long lifetimes increase the risk of exposure if a key is compromised.

Another important aspect of policy configuration is handling exceptions and bypasses. Not all traffic may require IPsec protection, and some services may be incompatible with encrypted communication. For example, certain diagnostic or monitoring tools may rely on examining packet contents, which are inaccessible when encrypted. Administrators must create exception rules that allow this traffic to flow without applying IPsec, while ensuring that these rules do not become vectors for attack or data leakage. Bypass policies must be carefully documented and reviewed to avoid unintended vulnerabilities.

Policy management extends beyond initial configuration. It involves ongoing monitoring, auditing, and adjustment to respond to changes in the network, emerging threats, and evolving business needs. Administrators must use logging and monitoring tools to verify that IPsec is functioning as expected, identify anomalies, and detect potential attacks. Regular audits of the SPD and SAD help ensure that policies remain aligned with organizational objectives and compliance obligations. As new applications are deployed or network topologies change, policies may need to be updated to accommodate new traffic patterns or integrate new endpoints.

Automation and orchestration tools can greatly enhance policy management in large-scale environments. By integrating IPsec policy configuration into centralized management platforms or software-defined networking solutions, administrators can apply consistent security policies across thousands of devices with minimal manual intervention. These tools can also use templates and profiles to enforce standard configurations, reducing the risk of human error and ensuring that best practices are uniformly applied. Integration with identity and access management systems allows policies to be dynamically applied based on user roles or device posture, enabling more granular and adaptive security.

In highly regulated environments, policy management must also address compliance and reporting requirements. IPsec policies must be documented, traceable, and demonstrably enforced. Audit logs showing which policies were in effect, which keys were used, and how traffic was protected may be required for compliance with standards such as GDPR, HIPAA, or PCI DSS. Policy changes must be reviewed and approved according to change management procedures, and rollback plans must be in place in case of misconfiguration or unexpected behavior.

Effective policy configuration also includes planning for high availability and fault tolerance. In critical environments, IPsec-enabled devices should be deployed in redundant configurations, with failover mechanisms that ensure continuity of secure communication in the event of device or link failure. Policies must be synchronized across redundant devices, and failover testing should be conducted regularly to validate the system's resilience. Scalability must also be considered, ensuring that the policy framework can support growth in the number of endpoints, users, and applications over time.

IPsec policy configuration and management is a multifaceted discipline that requires technical expertise, strategic planning, and continuous oversight. It is not enough to simply enable encryption; security must be thoughtfully designed, meticulously implemented, and vigilantly maintained. Through careful policy definition, algorithm selection, key management, exception handling, and proactive monitoring, administrators can harness the full power of IPsec to protect critical data and maintain trust in their network communications. The success of any IPsec deployment depends on the quality of its policy framework, making it a foundational element of enterprise network security.

IPsec in IPv6 Networks

IPsec plays a vital role in securing network communications, and its integration with IPv6 marks a significant evolution in how security is embedded into the architecture of modern networks. When IPv6 was developed to address the limitations of IPv4, particularly the exhaustion of IP address space and the need for more efficient routing, security was considered a core component of the new protocol. Unlike IPv4, where IPsec was optional and added after the fact, IPv6 was designed from the beginning to support IPsec natively. This intentional design choice positions IPsec as a fundamental building block for securing IPv6 communications, not just a feature to be bolted on when needed.

In the IPv6 architecture, IPsec is not just compatible—it is an inherent part of the protocol suite. The original specifications for IPv6 required IPsec support in all compliant implementations, although this requirement was later softened to improve deployment flexibility. Nevertheless, all major operating systems and network devices that support IPv6 are capable of using IPsec, and the protocol continues to be a preferred method for securing IPv6 traffic in enterprise and governmental networks. The primary components of IPsec— Authentication Header and Encapsulating Security Payload—operate in IPv6 just as they do in IPv4, providing data integrity, origin authentication, and encryption.

One of the key differences in using IPsec with IPv6 is how the protocol headers are structured. IPv6 introduces a new packet format with a simplified and more efficient header structure, using extension headers to carry optional information. This design makes it easier to insert IPsec headers into the packet without disrupting the core functionality of the protocol. The Authentication Header and ESP headers are implemented as IPv6 extension headers, which follow the main IPv6 header. This modularity streamlines packet processing and supports flexible placement of security features without the need for complex workarounds.

Because IPv6 addresses are vastly more abundant than those in IPv4, end-to-end connectivity is easier to achieve. This eliminates the widespread reliance on Network Address Translation, which was a common obstacle to IPsec deployment in IPv4 networks. NAT often interferes with IPsec's ability to authenticate packet headers, particularly when using the Authentication Header, because NAT modifies the source or destination address that AH attempts to validate. IPv6 eliminates this problem by restoring native end-to-end addressability, making IPsec easier to deploy and more reliable in IPv6 environments. The absence of NAT also simplifies troubleshooting and performance optimization in secured connections.

In IPv6 networks, IPsec is often used to secure traffic between two hosts, between gateways, or between a host and a gateway. These configurations can be implemented in transport or tunnel mode, depending on the requirements of the network. Transport mode is typically used for host-to-host communication, securing only the payload of the IP packet while leaving the original IPv6 header intact. Tunnel mode, on the other hand, is used to create secure tunnels between sites or networks. In this mode, the entire original packet is encapsulated within a new IPv6 packet, providing an additional layer of security and hiding the original source and destination addresses from potential attackers.

IPv6's built-in support for IPsec also aligns well with its other security features, such as Secure Neighbor Discovery, which protects against spoofing and man-in-the-middle attacks during the neighbor discovery process. While IPsec secures packet content, other IPv6 features focus on securing the control plane and the configuration of network elements. This layered approach creates a more comprehensive security posture, where multiple mechanisms work together to ensure both data confidentiality and infrastructure integrity.

Deploying IPsec in IPv6 networks still requires careful planning and policy management. Administrators must define Security Policies and Security Associations that determine which traffic will be protected and how. These policies are stored in the Security Policy Database and the Security Association Database, just as in IPv4 environments. The Internet Key Exchange protocol, especially IKEv2, is used to automate the negotiation and management of these associations. Because IPv6 allows for more flexible addressing and subnetting, administrators have more control over defining specific traffic selectors, such as which prefixes, ports, or protocols require IPsec protection.

Another benefit of IPsec in IPv6 networks is its suitability for large-scale enterprise and government deployments. Organizations that need to meet strict regulatory or compliance standards often use IPv6 with IPsec to ensure that sensitive data is encrypted and that communications are authenticated across multiple geographic regions. IPv6 also simplifies the process of assigning unique addresses to each device, which can be combined with IPsec to create device-specific security policies. This approach is useful for implementing granular access control and securing machine-to-machine communication in environments such as industrial automation, smart cities, and IoT systems.

Despite its advantages, IPsec in IPv6 does not automatically guarantee secure communication. It still requires deliberate configuration, maintenance, and monitoring. Misconfigured policies, weak cryptographic algorithms, and improper key management can all undermine the effectiveness of IPsec, regardless of the underlying protocol version. Additionally, because IPv6 adoption is still uneven across different regions and service providers, organizations must often support dual-stack environments where both IPv4 and IPv6 coexist. This dual-stack model can complicate IPsec deployment, requiring consistent policies and coordination across both protocols to ensure comprehensive protection.

Ongoing developments in IPv6 and IPsec continue to enhance their capabilities. The emergence of new cryptographic standards, the growth of software-defined networking, and the evolution of mobile and cloud-based infrastructure all influence how IPsec is used in IPv6 environments. For example, integration with modern identity and access management systems allows IPsec policies to be dynamically applied based on user roles or device attributes. Similarly, cloud providers are offering native support for IPv6 and IPsec in virtual private cloud configurations, making it easier to deploy secure, scalable solutions across hybrid environments.

As networks become more distributed and interconnected, the role of IPsec in IPv6 continues to expand. It provides a reliable and standardized way to secure communication without being tied to specific applications or devices. Its deep integration with the IPv6 protocol stack ensures that it can be applied consistently across various platforms and topologies. Whether protecting inter-site traffic, enabling secure remote access, or safeguarding machine communications in IoT deployments, IPsec in IPv6 networks remains a powerful tool for achieving end-to-end security in a world that increasingly depends on trusted digital communication.

SSL/TLS: An Introduction

SSL and TLS are cryptographic protocols designed to provide secure communication over computer networks, particularly the internet. SSL, which stands for Secure Sockets Layer, was the original protocol developed by Netscape in the mid-1990s. TLS, or Transport Layer Security, is its modern successor, developed by the Internet Engineering Task Force as a more secure and standardized version. Although SSL has been deprecated and is no longer considered secure, the term SSL is still commonly used when referring to TLS, especially in contexts such as SSL certificates or secure websites. Understanding how SSL and TLS work is essential for anyone involved in securing web communications, configuring servers, or managing data privacy in modern digital environments.

TLS operates between the application layer and the transport layer in the network stack, providing a secure channel over the inherently insecure TCP/IP protocols. The primary goals of TLS are to ensure the confidentiality, integrity, and authenticity of the data exchanged between a client and a server. Confidentiality is achieved through encryption, which prevents unauthorized parties from reading the contents of the communication. Integrity is maintained through message authentication codes, ensuring that the data has not been tampered with in transit. Authenticity is provided by digital certificates and public key infrastructure, confirming that the server (and optionally the client) is who it claims to be.

The most common use case for TLS is securing HTTP traffic, transforming it into HTTPS. When users visit a secure website, their browser and the web server initiate a process known as the TLS handshake. During this handshake, both parties agree on the cryptographic parameters to be used during the session. The handshake begins with the client sending a "ClientHello" message, which includes information such as the supported TLS versions, cipher suites, and a randomly generated number. The server responds with a "ServerHello" message, choosing the protocol version and cipher suite from the client's list and providing its digital certificate. This certificate contains the server's public key and is signed by a trusted Certificate Authority.

Once the client verifies the certificate and trusts the server's identity, the two parties perform key exchange using methods such as RSA or Diffie-Hellman. The purpose of this exchange is to establish a shared secret key that will be used to encrypt the session data. In modern implementations, forward secrecy is often used, meaning that even if the server's private key is later compromised, past session data remains secure. Once the key exchange is complete, both parties generate session keys from the shared secret and begin secure communication. All data exchanged from this point forward is encrypted and authenticated using the agreed-upon cipher suite.

TLS is not limited to web traffic. It is also used to secure email protocols such as IMAP, POP3, and SMTP, as well as file transfer protocols like FTPS and VPN tunnels using protocols such as OpenVPN. TLS is also employed in securing voice and messaging services, including VoIP and XMPP. Its widespread use and versatility have made it a cornerstone of modern internet security.

TLS versions have evolved over time to address vulnerabilities and improve performance. TLS 1.0 and 1.1 are now considered obsolete due to known security issues and have been largely phased out. TLS 1.2 introduced stronger cipher suites and allowed greater flexibility in choosing cryptographic algorithms. TLS 1.3, the most recent version, simplifies the handshake process, removes support for outdated and insecure algorithms, and significantly improves performance by reducing the number of round trips required to establish a secure session. TLS 1.3 also enforces forward secrecy by design, making it a more robust choice for protecting modern applications.

Despite its strong security guarantees, TLS is not immune to misconfiguration or implementation flaws. Common issues include using outdated protocol versions, weak cipher suites, self-signed certificates, and improper certificate validation. Attackers may exploit these weaknesses through methods such as downgrade attacks, where a client is tricked into using a less secure version of the protocol. Others may rely on certificate spoofing or man-in-the-middle attacks if certificate validation is improperly handled. To prevent these issues, administrators must follow best practices, such as disabling deprecated protocols, enabling only strong ciphers, and using certificates from trusted authorities.

Certificate management is another important aspect of TLS security. A digital certificate binds a public key to the identity of a server or user and is issued by a Certificate Authority, or CA. Browsers and operating systems maintain lists of trusted CAs, and only certificates signed by those authorities are considered valid. When a client connects to a server, it checks the server's certificate chain to ensure it can be traced back to a trusted root CA. Certificates are time-limited and must be renewed periodically. Automating this process using tools like Let's Encrypt and ACME clients helps ensure that certificates remain valid and reduces the risk of service disruption due to expiration.

In addition to securing data in transit, TLS also plays a role in establishing trust between parties. By verifying server identities and optionally client identities, TLS enables secure authentication without the need to expose passwords or other sensitive credentials in plaintext. Mutual TLS, or mTLS, is a variant where both the client and server present certificates, allowing for strong, two-way authentication. This is especially useful in enterprise environments and APIs where secure communication between systems must be verified on both ends.

TLS can also be integrated with other protocols to enhance security further. For instance, HTTP Strict Transport Security (HSTS) instructs browsers to only use HTTPS for communication with a particular domain, reducing the risk of downgrade attacks. Certificate Transparency is another initiative that requires certificates to be publicly logged, helping detect misissued or malicious certificates before they can be exploited.

As threats to internet security continue to evolve, TLS remains a critical line of defense. Its ability to provide a secure and authenticated channel for communication makes it indispensable in protecting online privacy and preventing data breaches. The protocol continues to adapt through the efforts of the security community and standardization bodies, ensuring it meets the growing demands of performance, compatibility, and resilience. Understanding how TLS functions, how to configure it correctly, and how to maintain a strong certificate infrastructure is essential for anyone responsible for securing digital communications in today's interconnected world.

The Evolution of SSL to TLS

The evolution of SSL to TLS is a significant chapter in the history of internet security, marking the progression from early efforts to encrypt web traffic to the modern cryptographic protocols that protect millions of online transactions every second. Secure Sockets Layer, or SSL, was originally developed by Netscape in the early 1990s as a way to secure communications between web browsers and servers. At that time, the internet was experiencing rapid growth, but most of its protocols transmitted data in plaintext, exposing users to a range of security threats such as eavesdropping, data manipulation, and identity theft. SSL was an ambitious attempt to address these issues by providing a secure channel that could authenticate parties and encrypt data in transit.

SSL 1.0 was never publicly released due to serious security flaws that were discovered internally during its development. SSL 2.0 was released in 1995 and became the first version of the protocol to see widespread use. However, SSL 2.0 suffered from multiple vulnerabilities and limitations. It lacked proper support for certificate-based authentication, had poor handling of cryptographic keys, and was susceptible to man-in-the-middle and cipher downgrade attacks. Additionally, SSL 2.0 did not support modern cryptographic algorithms, which made it weak against the increasingly sophisticated attacks of the time. As a result, SSL 2.0 was quickly replaced by SSL 3.0, which was introduced later the same year with significant improvements in protocol structure and security mechanisms.

SSL 3.0 addressed many of the shortcomings of its predecessor by introducing stronger cryptographic protections, better support for digital certificates, and a more flexible handshake protocol that allowed for secure negotiation of encryption and authentication parameters. It became the foundation for what would eventually evolve into TLS. Despite its enhancements, SSL 3.0 still had design issues that were difficult to fix without a complete overhaul of the protocol. One of its most notable weaknesses, later discovered, was its vulnerability to the POODLE attack, which exploited the way SSL 3.0 handled block cipher padding. This vulnerability demonstrated that the protocol could no longer be trusted to protect data, prompting the security community to push for a transition to its successor.

In 1999, the Internet Engineering Task Force introduced Transport Layer Security, or TLS, as the official successor to SSL. TLS 1.0 was based heavily on SSL 3.0, but with important changes that made it more secure and standards-compliant. The differences included more robust message authentication using HMAC, improved key derivation functions, and tighter control over the negotiation of cryptographic algorithms. Although TLS 1.0 retained backward compatibility with SSL 3.0 to ease adoption, its internal mechanisms were more thoroughly vetted and designed to resist known attack vectors. This marked the beginning of a new era in secure communications, where cryptographic protocols would be held to a higher standard of formal review and global coordination.

Over time, TLS itself underwent several revisions to address new security challenges and adapt to the evolving landscape of internet technologies. TLS 1.1 was introduced in 2006 to fix a few known issues in TLS 1.0, including the addition of protection against cipher block chaining (CBC) attacks. It also improved support for initialization vectors and error handling during handshake failures. While TLS 1.1 represented progress, it was not widely adopted because the industry was already preparing for more substantial improvements that would come with TLS 1.2.

TLS 1.2, released in 2008, became the dominant version of the protocol for over a decade. It introduced significant changes to the cryptographic flexibility of TLS by allowing clients and servers to negotiate a wide range of algorithms and key exchange methods. TLS 1.2 enabled support for modern cipher suites like AES-GCM and introduced the ability to use stronger hash functions for message authentication, such as SHA-256 and SHA-384. These improvements enhanced both the performance and security of encrypted communications. TLS 1.2 also offered better support for secure renegotiation and added protections against a variety of attacks that had been discovered since the release of TLS 1.0 and 1.1. Its widespread adoption made it the de facto standard for securing web traffic, email, voice, and other internet-based services.

The next major evolution came with the release of TLS 1.3 in 2018. This version was a complete redesign of the protocol with security and performance as the primary goals. TLS 1.3 removed many legacy features that had become liabilities, such as support for outdated algorithms like RC4, MD5, and SHA-1. It eliminated the ability to fall back to older protocol versions, thereby reducing the risk of downgrade attacks. One of the most significant changes in TLS 1.3 was the simplification of the handshake process, which reduced the number of round trips required to establish a secure session. This improvement not only enhanced performance, particularly for mobile and high-latency environments, but also reduced the attack surface by removing unnecessary complexity. TLS 1.3 also mandated forward secrecy, meaning that even if long-term keys are compromised in the future, past communications remain secure.

As TLS continued to mature, the use of SSL was gradually deprecated. SSL 2.0 was officially deprecated in 2011, and SSL 3.0 followed in 2015. Major web browsers, operating systems, and cloud providers began removing support for SSL entirely, and organizations were encouraged to upgrade their infrastructure to use only secure versions of TLS. Even older versions of TLS, such as 1.0 and 1.1, were eventually declared obsolete and removed from many platforms due to their inadequate security and the availability of better alternatives.

The transition from SSL to TLS has not only been about upgrading technology but also about establishing best practices for secure communication. The widespread adoption of TLS certificates, the enforcement of HTTPS across the web, and the development of new protocols like HTTP/2 and HTTP/3 have all relied on the underlying strength and trustworthiness of TLS. The protocol has become a critical component of the internet's security infrastructure, enabling safe online banking, shopping, email, messaging, and countless other services that require confidentiality and integrity.

The evolution of SSL to TLS reflects the broader journey of cybersecurity as a discipline. It demonstrates how standards evolve in response to emerging threats, how collaboration between industry and academia leads to stronger technologies, and how security must continually adapt to meet the demands of a rapidly changing digital world. As TLS continues to evolve and new versions are developed to respond to future challenges, it remains a cornerstone of trust in the digital age, built upon decades of learning, refinement, and innovation.

TLS Protocol Layers and Structure

Transport Layer Security, commonly referred to as TLS, is a cryptographic protocol that provides secure communication over computer networks. It is widely used to protect data in transit, ensuring confidentiality, integrity, and authenticity between communicating applications. To achieve these goals, TLS is composed of multiple layers, each responsible for a specific function within the overall protocol. Understanding the structure of TLS and how its layers interact is essential to grasp how secure communication is established and maintained in a wide range of online activities, from browsing websites and sending emails to using mobile apps and conducting online banking.

The architecture of TLS is modular, consisting of a set of layered protocols that work together to provide security services. At the lowest level of the TLS stack is the record protocol, which serves as the foundation for all higher-level TLS functions. The record protocol is responsible for fragmenting application data into manageable blocks, compressing it (if compression is enabled), applying a message authentication code for integrity, encrypting the data for confidentiality, and then transmitting the resulting ciphertext to the peer. On the receiving end, the record protocol reverses these operations, verifying the authenticity of the data and decrypting it before delivering it to the application.

The record protocol handles both application data and control messages. When application data is being transmitted, such as a web page from a server to a browser, it is encapsulated within the TLS record format and protected according to the parameters established during the handshake. Control messages, which manage the state and operation of the TLS session, are also sent via the record protocol. These include alerts that notify the peer about errors or connection closure, as well as handshake messages that are critical to establishing the secure session.

Above the record layer sits the handshake protocol, which is arguably the most important component of TLS. This protocol is responsible for establishing the security parameters of a session, including negotiating the version of TLS to use, selecting cryptographic algorithms, authenticating the server and optionally the client, and generating the shared keys that will be used for encryption and authentication. The handshake begins with a client sending a "ClientHello" message that lists supported TLS versions, cipher suites, compression methods, and other relevant data. The server replies with a "ServerHello" message that selects the appropriate parameters and provides its digital certificate.

The handshake protocol also includes the exchange of key materials. Depending on the selected cipher suite, this may involve public key encryption, ephemeral Diffie-Hellman key exchange, or elliptic curve variants. The goal is to derive a shared secret between the client and server that can be used to generate symmetric session keys. These keys are then used by the record protocol to protect data. Modern versions of TLS, particularly TLS 1.3, emphasize forward secrecy by using ephemeral key exchange methods that ensure session keys are never reused and that past sessions remain secure even if long-term private keys are compromised in the future.

One key aspect of the handshake is the authentication of the server using a digital certificate issued by a trusted Certificate Authority. The certificate contains the server's public key and identifies the server's domain. The client verifies the certificate's validity by checking its signature against a list of trusted root CAs. If the certificate is valid and trusted, the client proceeds with the handshake. In mutual authentication scenarios, the server may also request a certificate from the client, allowing both parties to authenticate each other. Once authentication and key exchange are complete, the client and server send "Finished" messages encrypted with the newly negotiated keys, signaling the end of the handshake and the beginning of secure data exchange.

The alert protocol operates alongside the record and handshake protocols. It is used to signal errors or to indicate changes in connection state. Alerts are categorized as either warning or fatal. A warning may indicate a recoverable issue or inform the peer about a non-critical condition. A fatal alert, however, indicates a serious problem and causes the connection to be terminated immediately. Common alert messages include "unexpected_message," "bad_record_mac," "handshake_failure," and "close_notify." The use of alerts allows TLS implementations to respond to problems gracefully and in a secure manner.

TLS also supports a change cipher spec protocol, which is a single-message protocol used during the handshake. When sent, it signals that all subsequent messages will be protected using the negotiated cipher suite and keys. This protocol marks the transition from unencrypted to encrypted communication and is a key step in the successful establishment of a secure session.

TLS's layered structure is designed to be both secure and flexible. By separating concerns across different protocols—record, handshake, alert, and change cipher spec—TLS can evolve each component independently as new security requirements emerge. This modularity also makes it easier to identify and address vulnerabilities, ensuring that implementations can adapt to advances in cryptography and evolving threat models.

TLS 1.3, the latest version of the protocol, simplifies the handshake by removing obsolete and insecure features. It eliminates support for older algorithms and reduces the number of round trips required to establish a session, improving both security and performance. TLS 1.3 combines some previously distinct layers and functions for efficiency but retains the same conceptual framework. It also mandates encryption earlier in the handshake process, ensuring that more of the negotiation remains confidential and protected from eavesdropping.

Each TLS session is also associated with a session state, which includes the negotiated parameters, keys, and other contextual information. In earlier versions of TLS, session resumption was managed through session IDs or session tickets, allowing clients to reconnect to servers without repeating the full handshake. In TLS 1.3, session resumption is handled through pre-shared keys, which further enhance performance while maintaining security. These mechanisms reduce latency and server load, especially in high-traffic environments.

In practice, the layered structure of TLS ensures that applications using it, such as web browsers, email clients, and messaging platforms, can rely on a robust and proven framework for secure communication. Developers using TLS do not need to manage encryption directly; instead, they use high-level libraries or APIs that implement the protocol's layers internally. This abstraction allows developers to focus on application logic while benefiting from strong, standards-based security.

TLS protocol layers and structure represent a culmination of decades of cryptographic research and real-world testing. Its careful design balances security, performance, and compatibility, making it one of the most widely adopted security protocols in existence. Through its layered approach, TLS offers a powerful yet adaptable foundation for protecting the confidentiality, authenticity, and integrity of digital communications in an increasingly connected world.

Handshake Protocol in TLS

The handshake protocol in TLS is a fundamental process that initiates a secure communication session between two parties, typically a client and a server. This protocol is responsible for negotiating the security parameters of a session, verifying identities through certificates, and generating shared keys that will be used to encrypt and authenticate the data exchanged over the network. The handshake occurs at the beginning of a TLS session and lays the groundwork for all secure communication that follows. Without the handshake, it would be impossible to establish a confidential and authenticated channel over an inherently insecure medium like the internet.

The handshake protocol is layered on top of the record protocol and relies on a series of structured messages exchanged between the client and the server. These messages follow a strict sequence and carry essential data that helps both sides agree on how to communicate securely. One of the key objectives of the handshake is to determine which version of TLS to use. This is important because newer versions offer better security and performance, but the client and server must both support the chosen version. During the handshake, the client sends a message called ClientHello, which includes the highest version of TLS it supports, a list of supported cipher suites, compression methods, and other options such as supported extensions. It also includes a randomly generated number known as the client random.

Upon receiving the ClientHello, the server responds with a ServerHello message. This message confirms the TLS version that will be used for the session, selects a cipher suite from the list offered by the client, and includes the server's own randomly generated number, known as the server random. The server also sends its digital certificate, which contains its public key and is signed by a trusted Certificate Authority. This certificate is used by the client to verify the server's identity, helping prevent impersonation and man-in-the-middle attacks. If mutual authentication is required, the server can request a certificate from the client as well.

After the exchange of random numbers and certificates, the next step involves the key exchange process. The exact method depends on the cipher suite selected. In traditional RSA-based handshakes, the client would generate a pre-master secret and encrypt it using the server's public key, then send it to the server. However, modern TLS implementations prefer ephemeral Diffie-Hellman or elliptic-curve Diffie-Hellman key exchanges, which provide forward secrecy. Forward secrecy ensures that even if long-term keys are compromised at some point in the future, past session keys remain protected and cannot be retroactively decrypted.

Once the key exchange is complete, both the client and server independently derive the same session keys using the shared secret and the previously exchanged random numbers. These keys are then used to create encryption and authentication keys for the secure session. Before secure communication begins, both parties send a Finished message, which is the first message encrypted with the new session keys. This message includes a hash of all previous handshake messages, providing a final integrity check. If either side detects any inconsistency, the handshake fails and the connection is terminated.

The handshake protocol also supports the use of extensions that allow additional capabilities to be negotiated. For instance, Server Name Indication allows the client to specify the hostname it is trying to connect to, which is useful in environments where multiple services share the same IP address. Another important extension is Application-Layer Protocol Negotiation, which allows the client and server to agree on the application protocol to be used over the secure connection, such as HTTP/2 or HTTP/3. Extensions have become essential to the adaptability of TLS, allowing the protocol to evolve without breaking compatibility.

With the release of TLS 1.3, the handshake protocol was significantly streamlined to improve both security and performance. TLS 1.3 removed many older features that had become security liabilities, such as support for RSA key exchange and static Diffie-Hellman. The number of round trips required to complete the handshake was also reduced, making it possible to establish a secure session with fewer messages. In ideal conditions, TLS 1.3 can complete the handshake in a single round trip, and when session resumption is used, it can even achieve zero round-trip time, allowing encrypted data to be sent immediately. These enhancements make TLS 1.3 faster and more secure than previous versions.

TLS 1.3 also introduced changes to the way handshake messages are encrypted. In earlier versions, most of the handshake was conducted in plaintext, which exposed metadata and allowed for certain types of passive attacks. In TLS 1.3, encryption begins earlier in the handshake process, making it more difficult for attackers to analyze or manipulate the messages. By encrypting sensitive parts of the handshake, TLS 1.3 improves privacy and reduces the protocol's susceptibility to inspection and interference.

Despite its improvements, the handshake protocol remains a complex process that requires careful implementation. Mistakes in the handling of certificates, key exchanges, or protocol negotiation can lead to serious security vulnerabilities. Attackers may attempt to exploit poorly configured servers by forcing a downgrade to a weaker cipher suite or protocol version. To prevent this, TLS implementations must validate every step of the handshake, enforce strict version checks, and reject insecure or outdated options.

The handshake protocol also plays a crucial role in certificate validation. When a server presents its certificate, the client must verify that it is signed by a trusted Certificate Authority, that it has not expired, and that it matches the domain name being requested. Failure to validate these properties correctly can lead to impersonation attacks. Some clients also check certificate revocation status using methods like OCSP or CRLs to ensure that compromised certificates are not accepted.

Beyond technical functionality, the handshake protocol enables trust. It allows users to feel confident that they are communicating with the right service and that their data is being protected. Every time a person visits a secure website, sends a private message, or accesses an encrypted email, the handshake protocol is working behind the scenes to create a foundation of trust. Its design reflects decades of cryptographic research and real-world experience, balancing performance and security in an environment that is constantly evolving.

The handshake protocol in TLS is more than just a series of technical steps. It is the negotiation of trust between two parties, the establishment of privacy in an open network, and the mechanism by which the modern internet maintains its security. From its first message to the final confirmation of encrypted communication, the TLS handshake sets the stage for secure and reliable digital interactions across the globe.

Cipher Suites and TLS Negotiation

Cipher suites and TLS negotiation are central to the operation of the Transport Layer Security protocol. These components determine how two parties—typically a client and a server—will secure their communication channel. A cipher suite in the context of TLS is a named collection of cryptographic algorithms that define how secure communication will occur during and after the handshake. TLS negotiation is the process through which the client and server agree upon the most suitable cipher suite to use for a particular session. The selection of cipher suites and the negotiation process are critical for ensuring that the security and performance of encrypted communication meet modern standards and resist evolving threats.

When a client initiates a TLS session, it sends a message called ClientHello, which includes a list of supported cipher suites in the order of preference. Each cipher suite in that list is a combination of algorithms used for key exchange, authentication, encryption, and message authentication. The server, upon receiving this list, selects a cipher suite from those offered by the client and responds with a ServerHello message indicating the chosen suite. This negotiation ensures compatibility between the two parties while allowing both to prioritize algorithms they support or trust. A mismatch in capabilities or support can lead to the session being terminated, so both parties must have at least one cipher suite in common for the handshake to succeed.

Cipher suites are named using a standardized format that describes the components included. For example, a cipher suite might be represented as TLS_ECDHE_RSA_WITH_AES_128_GCM_SHA256. This name indicates that the session will use Elliptic Curve Diffie-Hellman Ephemeral (ECDHE) for key exchange, RSA for authentication, AES with a 128-bit key in Galois/Counter Mode for encryption, and SHA-256 for the message authentication code. Each component plays a role in ensuring a different aspect of security. The key exchange mechanism determines how the shared secret is generated. The authentication algorithm verifies the identity of the parties. The encryption algorithm protects the confidentiality of the data, and the MAC algorithm ensures the data's integrity.

Key exchange mechanisms such as RSA and Diffie-Hellman are crucial to securely negotiating session keys. RSA was widely used in early TLS versions but has gradually been replaced by forward-secret algorithms like Ephemeral Diffie-Hellman and its elliptic curve variant, ECDHE. These modern algorithms generate unique session keys for each connection, preventing past communications from being decrypted if long-term keys are compromised. Forward secrecy is now considered a best practice and is mandatory in TLS 1.3, reflecting the industry's move toward stronger, more resilient cryptographic techniques.

Authentication methods within cipher suites typically rely on public key infrastructure. The server provides a digital certificate during the handshake that contains a public key. The client uses this key to validate the server's identity. The choice of authentication algorithm, such as RSA or ECDSA, affects the type of key included in the certificate. RSA has long been the standard, but elliptic curve algorithms like ECDSA offer equivalent security with shorter key lengths, improving performance and reducing computational overhead.

Encryption algorithms define how data is encrypted for confidentiality. TLS supports several types, but the industry has moved away from outdated methods such as RC4 and 3DES due to known vulnerabilities. Modern cipher suites use the Advanced Encryption Standard, or AES, often in modes like Galois/Counter Mode for both security and efficiency. GCM provides both encryption and integrity verification in a single step, streamlining the record layer processing. Some suites also support ChaCha20-Poly1305, a cipher designed for environments where hardware acceleration of AES is not available. ChaCha20 is especially popular on mobile devices and in certain high-performance web applications because of its speed and resistance to side-channel attacks.

The MAC algorithm ensures that each message sent over the TLS session has not been altered in transit. This is achieved by generating a cryptographic checksum that the receiving party verifies. In older TLS versions, MACs like HMAC-SHA1 were common, but due to weaknesses in SHA-1, newer suites prefer stronger hashes like HMAC-SHA256 or integrated AEAD modes like those used in AES-GCM and ChaCha20-Poly1305, which combine encryption and integrity in a single operation.

TLS 1.2 supports a wide variety of cipher suites and allows clients and servers to choose from among them during the handshake. However, this flexibility can also lead to misconfigurations, where servers support weak or outdated suites that attackers can exploit. Downgrade attacks, for instance, involve tricking a client or server into using a less secure cipher suite than both actually support. Mitigation mechanisms such as downgrade protection flags and secure renegotiation help reduce this risk, but administrators must carefully configure their systems to disable obsolete suites and enforce strong defaults.

TLS 1.3, introduced in 2018, made substantial changes to cipher suite definitions and the negotiation process. It removed support for many legacy algorithms and streamlined the list of supported suites. In TLS 1.3, cipher suites no longer include separate fields for key exchange and authentication; these functions are handled independently earlier in the handshake. A TLS 1.3 cipher suite includes only the symmetric encryption algorithm and the hash function used for message authentication. For example, a TLS 1.3 cipher suite might be named TLS_AES_128_GCM_SHA256, indicating that AES in GCM mode will be used with SHA-256. This simplification reduces confusion and limits the possibility of insecure combinations, resulting in stronger overall security.

TLS 1.3 also removed features like static RSA key exchange and all forms of non-ephemeral Diffie-Hellman, enforcing the use of forward-secret methods. Additionally, session resumption and early data (0-RTT) were redesigned to provide better performance without compromising security. These changes reflect a broader philosophy of minimalism and clarity in protocol design, aiming to prevent misconfiguration and eliminate insecure practices.

Selecting the right cipher suites for a TLS implementation requires balancing security and compatibility. Administrators should ensure that only strong, modern suites are enabled, prioritize forward secrecy, and monitor security advisories for updates on cryptographic standards. Public-facing services, in particular, should be audited regularly to confirm that they do not support deprecated algorithms or weak configurations.

Cipher suites and their negotiation define the security boundaries of every TLS session. They represent the choices that shape the strength of the encryption, the trust in identity, and the resilience of the connection against modern threats. As protocols like TLS continue to evolve, understanding cipher suites and their role in secure negotiation remains an essential skill for anyone involved in maintaining the security of networked systems. From the moment a connection is initiated to the end of a secure session, cipher suites are the mechanisms that guard the integrity and privacy of data in motion.

TLS Session Management and Resumption

TLS session management and resumption are essential components of the Transport Layer Security protocol, designed to improve the efficiency and performance of secure communication. Establishing a secure TLS session involves a complex handshake process that requires several steps to negotiate cryptographic parameters, exchange certificates, and generate session keys. While this initial handshake is necessary to ensure a high level of security, repeating it for every new connection between the same client and server would introduce significant latency and computational overhead. To address this issue, TLS includes mechanisms for session management and resumption, allowing parties to reuse previously negotiated security parameters under certain conditions.

A TLS session begins when a client initiates a handshake with a server. During this process, both parties agree on the cipher suite, exchange certificates if necessary, and establish shared session keys. Once the handshake is complete, the session enters an active state and both the client and server retain session-specific information, such as session identifiers, encryption keys, and negotiated options. This session data enables the secure exchange of application data using symmetric encryption, which is much faster than public key operations.

To avoid repeating the full handshake each time a connection is established, TLS supports two main methods of session resumption: session ID-based resumption and session ticket-based resumption. These techniques reduce the computational cost of establishing new sessions, minimize handshake latency, and improve the user experience, especially in applications that require frequent or repeated secure connections such as web browsing, email access, or API calls.

In session ID-based resumption, the server assigns a unique identifier to each TLS session and sends it to the client during the initial handshake. The client stores this session ID and can later present it to the server when attempting to reconnect. If the server still has the session parameters associated with that ID in its cache, it can skip the full handshake and resume the session using the previously agreed-upon keys. This method requires the server to maintain a session cache and match incoming session IDs with stored session data. While effective, this approach has scalability limitations, as servers must allocate memory and resources to track potentially thousands or millions of session IDs.

To overcome the limitations of server-side caching, TLS also supports session ticket-based resumption. In this method, the server generates an encrypted session ticket that contains all the necessary session information and sends it to the client. The ticket is encrypted using a key known only to the server, ensuring that its contents cannot be modified or read by the client or an attacker. When the client reconnects, it presents the session ticket instead of a session ID. The server decrypts the ticket, retrieves the session information, and resumes the session if it is still valid. Because the session state is stored on the client side, this approach is more scalable and stateless from the server's perspective, making it particularly well-suited for large-scale deployments such as content delivery networks and cloud services.

Both session ID and session ticket methods reduce the number of round trips and computational steps required to re-establish a secure connection. This is particularly valuable in scenarios where latency is critical, such as mobile applications or services accessed over high-latency networks. By avoiding repeated public key operations and certificate verifications, session resumption helps improve performance while maintaining the security of the communication channel.

TLS 1.3 introduced further improvements to session management and resumption. Unlike earlier versions, TLS 1.3 does not use session IDs. Instead, it relies solely on Pre-Shared Keys, or PSKs, which are derived from previous handshakes and used for session resumption. In this model, the server issues a resumption ticket during the initial handshake. This ticket includes the cryptographic material necessary to derive a PSK and is encrypted to prevent tampering. When the client reconnects, it uses the PSK to initiate a new handshake. If the server recognizes and accepts the PSK, it proceeds with an abbreviated handshake that skips certain steps, such as key exchange and certificate validation. This not only reduces the number of messages exchanged but also allows for 0-RTT (zero round trip time) resumption, where the client can begin sending encrypted data immediately, without waiting for the server's reply.

0-RTT resumption offers significant performance benefits, but it also introduces new security challenges. Since the client sends data before receiving confirmation from the server, replay attacks become a concern. An attacker could potentially capture and replay 0-RTT data to the server under certain conditions. To mitigate this risk, 0-RTT is typically restricted to idempotent operations, and servers must implement replay protection mechanisms such as storing hashes of recently received messages. TLS 1.3 makes these trade-offs explicit and allows administrators to choose whether or not to enable 0-RTT based on their application's risk profile.

Effective session management in TLS requires careful handling of session lifetimes, ticket expiration, and key rotation. Session tickets and PSKs should be short-lived to reduce the window of opportunity for attackers and to ensure that cryptographic keys are refreshed regularly. Servers should rotate the keys used to encrypt session tickets and invalidate old tickets when the key is changed. Additionally, clients should avoid caching session information indefinitely and must be able to fall back to a full handshake if a resumption attempt fails.

Proper implementation and management of these mechanisms are crucial to maintaining a balance between performance and security.

TLS session resumption also plays a critical role in maintaining secure connections in mobile and intermittent environments. In scenarios where devices frequently switch networks or experience brief connectivity interruptions, session resumption allows them to quickly re-establish secure communication without restarting the handshake from scratch. This capability is vital for real-time applications such as messaging, voice communication, and streaming media, where minimizing delay is essential for user satisfaction.

The use of TLS session resumption is widely supported across modern web browsers, servers, and libraries. Developers can enable and customize resumption behavior through configuration settings and APIs, allowing them to tailor the security and performance characteristics of their applications. However, developers and system administrators must also stay informed about the evolving security landscape, as new vulnerabilities and attack techniques may influence best practices for session management.

TLS session management and resumption form the backbone of scalable and responsive secure communications. By allowing clients and servers to securely reuse cryptographic parameters from previous sessions, these features reduce latency, conserve computational resources, and enable seamless connectivity in dynamic environments. When implemented and managed correctly, they preserve the integrity and confidentiality of communications while delivering the speed and reliability that modern users and applications demand. As internet security continues to evolve, session resumption remains a crucial element of TLS, demonstrating the protocol's adaptability to the changing needs of global digital infrastructure.

Certificate-Based Authentication in TLS

Certificate-based authentication in TLS is one of the foundational elements that makes secure communication over the internet possible. At its core, this mechanism ensures that one or both parties involved in a TLS session are who they claim to be. Without some form of identity verification, encrypted communication would be vulnerable to man-in-the-middle attacks, where malicious actors could impersonate a server or client to intercept or manipulate traffic. Digital certificates serve as digital passports that provide a verifiable link between a public cryptographic key and the identity of an entity such as a website, organization, or user. This process is fundamental not only for securing websites but also for enabling trust in applications, email systems, APIs, and enterprise networks.

In most typical TLS scenarios, such as when a user visits a secure website using HTTPS, only the server is authenticated using a certificate. The client initiates a handshake by sending a ClientHello message to the server. In response, the server provides a ServerHello message, along with a digital certificate that contains its public key. This certificate is issued by a trusted Certificate Authority, known as a CA, which vouches for the legitimacy of the server's identity. The client then validates the certificate to determine whether it should trust the server. This validation process involves checking the digital signature of the certificate, verifying the certificate chain up to a trusted root, ensuring the certificate has not expired, and confirming that the domain name in the certificate matches the server's address.

The concept of a certificate chain is central to this trust model. Certificates are typically issued in a hierarchical structure, where a root CA signs intermediate CA certificates, and those intermediates in turn sign the certificates of end-entities such as websites. This hierarchy enables scalability and delegation of trust without requiring every entity to be directly signed by a root authority. Clients, such as browsers or operating systems, maintain a list of trusted root certificates. When a server presents a certificate, the client checks that it can build a valid chain from the presented certificate to one of its trusted roots. If the chain cannot be validated, the connection is either rejected or marked as insecure, depending on the client's policies.

Another critical aspect of certificate validation is revocation checking. Even a certificate issued by a trusted CA may need to be invalidated before its expiration date due to compromise or other issues. TLS clients can check whether a certificate has been revoked using mechanisms such as the Certificate Revocation List (CRL) or the

Online Certificate Status Protocol (OCSP). A CRL is a list of revoked certificates published by a CA, while OCSP allows real-time status queries about a specific certificate. Both mechanisms help mitigate the risks of relying on compromised or misused certificates, although they introduce complexity and potential performance trade-offs.

While server authentication is the most common use of certificates in TLS, the protocol also supports client authentication. In mutual TLS, or mTLS, the server requests a certificate from the client during the handshake. The client presents its certificate, and the server validates it just as the client validates the server's certificate. This bidirectional verification provides a higher level of trust and is particularly useful in enterprise environments, API security, and machine-to-machine communication, where access must be restricted to known and trusted identities. Client certificates are typically issued by a private or internal CA and can be tied to specific users, devices, or applications, enabling fine-grained access control.

To support certificate-based authentication, the TLS protocol relies on public key infrastructure, or PKI. PKI encompasses the set of roles, policies, hardware, software, and procedures needed to create, manage, distribute, use, store, and revoke digital certificates. CAs are the most visible part of PKI, but the full system also includes registration authorities that verify identity information before a certificate is issued, as well as certificate repositories and validation tools. Secure certificate management is essential for maintaining the trust and reliability of TLS. Weak key generation, poor handling of private keys, or improper storage of certificates can lead to serious vulnerabilities.

The digital certificate itself is structured according to standards such as X.509, which defines the format and contents of the certificate. An X.509 certificate includes fields such as the subject's name, the issuer's name, the public key, a serial number, the certificate's validity period, and extensions such as the Subject Alternative Name, which allows multiple domains to be covered by a single certificate. The certificate is signed by the CA using its private key, and this signature can be verified using the CA's public key. The presence of a valid digital signature indicates that the certificate has not been tampered with and was indeed issued by the trusted authority.

In practice, the use of certificates and PKI is supported by widely used protocols and standards. The Automatic Certificate Management Environment, or ACME, has simplified certificate issuance and renewal, enabling services like Let's Encrypt to offer free, automated certificates to millions of websites. This has dramatically increased the adoption of HTTPS and made certificate-based TLS authentication more accessible to developers and organizations of all sizes. ACME clients run on servers and handle the challenge-response process that proves domain ownership before a certificate is issued.

Despite the robustness of the certificate-based model, there have been incidents that highlight its vulnerabilities. Cases where trusted CAs issued fraudulent certificates, either due to compromise or mismanagement, have led to major disruptions and security concerns. As a result, the ecosystem has developed additional safeguards, including Certificate Transparency logs, which are public, tamper-evident records of certificate issuance. These logs help detect unauthorized or unexpected certificates and allow domain owners and security researchers to monitor and audit the activity of CAs.

In modern security architectures, certificate-based authentication continues to expand beyond web applications. It is increasingly used in securing APIs, enabling single sign-on solutions, managing access in cloud and hybrid environments, and securing communications between microservices. With the rise of zero-trust models, where every entity must be verified before access is granted, the ability to authenticate identities based on trusted certificates becomes even more critical. Whether embedded in smart devices, integrated into VPNs, or used to protect Kubernetes clusters, certificate-based TLS authentication provides a versatile and scalable method for establishing digital trust.

Certificate-based authentication in TLS is a sophisticated and essential mechanism that underpins much of the internet's security. It provides a cryptographically secure method of verifying identity and establishing trust, allowing users to communicate, transact, and share data with confidence. By relying on well-established standards, managed trust hierarchies, and robust validation procedures, this system continues to evolve in response to new threats and new technological demands. Its continued development and integration into modern systems ensure that secure communication remains both trustworthy and practical in a digital world that increasingly depends on privacy and authentication.

TLS Record Protocol

The TLS Record Protocol is a fundamental component of the Transport Layer Security (TLS) protocol, responsible for providing secure and reliable communication over a network. It operates beneath the higher-level TLS protocols such as the handshake, alert, and change cipher spec protocols, and above the transport layer, typically TCP. The Record Protocol ensures that data is transmitted securely by applying confidentiality through encryption, integrity through message authentication, and proper segmentation for efficient transmission. Its design allows TLS to be both secure and flexible, capable of supporting a wide variety of applications ranging from web browsing to email and beyond.

The primary function of the TLS Record Protocol is to take data from higher-level protocols or applications and prepare it for secure transmission. This involves a series of steps that include fragmentation, optional compression, message authentication, and encryption. Each of these steps contributes to the overall security and performance of the TLS session. When data is received from the application layer, the Record Protocol first fragments the data into manageable blocks. These blocks are then optionally compressed, although in modern TLS versions, compression is generally disabled to prevent certain types of attacks such as the CRIME attack, which exploit predictable patterns in compressed data.

After fragmentation and optional compression, the Record Protocol adds a Message Authentication Code (MAC) to ensure integrity and authenticity. The MAC is generated using a cryptographic hash function, such as SHA-256, combined with a secret key known only to the communicating parties. This MAC allows the receiver to verify that the data has not been tampered with in transit and that it originated from a trusted source. In versions of TLS that use authenticated encryption with associated data (AEAD) modes, such as AES-GCM or

ChaCha20-Poly1305, the MAC is integrated with the encryption process rather than being added as a separate field. AEAD modes provide both encryption and authentication in a single, efficient operation, improving both security and performance.

The final step in preparing data for transmission is encryption. The Record Protocol encrypts the entire block of data, including the MAC if used separately, using the negotiated encryption algorithm and session keys established during the TLS handshake. This encryption ensures that the data remains confidential and cannot be read by unauthorized parties. Once encrypted, the data is encapsulated in a TLS record, which includes a header specifying the record type, the TLS version, and the length of the payload. This header is sent in plaintext so that the receiving system can process the record correctly, even before decryption.

When the record is received by the other party, the process is reversed. The receiver uses the header to determine how to process the record, decrypts the data using the session key, verifies the MAC or performs AEAD validation, decompresses the payload if compression was used, and finally reassembles the original data. If any of these steps fail, such as a MAC mismatch or decryption error, the record is discarded, and an alert may be sent to the peer indicating the failure. This strict verification ensures that tampered or corrupted data is not passed on to the application, maintaining the integrity of the session.

One of the strengths of the TLS Record Protocol is its independence from the specific data being transmitted. It treats all content, whether it is part of the handshake, application data, or control messages, in the same way. Each record is self-contained and processed individually, which enhances both reliability and scalability. This modularity also allows TLS to support different types of higher-level protocols and applications without requiring changes to the underlying security mechanisms. The Record Protocol is responsible only for the secure delivery of data, not for understanding its content, making it a versatile component of the overall TLS architecture.

TLS uses specific record types to differentiate between the kinds of data being transmitted. For example, a record type of 22 indicates that the payload contains handshake messages, while a type of 23 indicates application data. This classification helps the receiving system interpret the data correctly after decryption. Alert messages, which signal problems or indicate session closure, also use their own record type. The separation of different types of content into distinct records enhances clarity and organization within the TLS session.

TLS versions have refined the Record Protocol to improve security and performance. In TLS 1.2, the Record Protocol supports both traditional cipher block chaining (CBC) encryption with separate MACs and AEAD cipher modes. However, CBC mode is known to be vulnerable to padding oracle attacks if not implemented correctly. TLS 1.3 eliminates support for CBC entirely and mandates the use of AEAD ciphers. Additionally, TLS 1.3 reduces the overhead of the Record Protocol by encrypting more handshake data earlier in the process and simplifying the structure of records. These changes reflect a broader trend toward streamlining and hardening the protocol against modern threats.

Another important consideration in the Record Protocol is the handling of record size. While the protocol allows for records of varying length, excessively large records can introduce latency and memory usage issues, while very small records can lead to inefficiency due to increased header overhead. Implementations must strike a balance that ensures optimal throughput without compromising security or responsiveness. Some advanced techniques, such as record splitting, are used to mitigate attacks on specific cipher modes, though these techniques are no longer necessary in TLS 1.3 due to the use of safer ciphers.

Sequence numbers are also a critical part of the Record Protocol, though they are not transmitted as part of the record itself. Each side of a TLS session maintains its own sequence number counter, incrementing it with each record sent. The sequence number is used as part of the MAC or AEAD input, binding the message to its place in the communication stream. This helps prevent reordering, replay, or injection of records by attackers. If sequence numbers get out of sync due to packet loss or tampering, the session will fail to validate and will be terminated, preserving the integrity of the communication.

The TLS Record Protocol is a highly effective mechanism for securing data in transit. By providing encryption, authentication, and integrity in a structured and extensible format, it serves as the foundation for all other TLS functionality. Whether protecting a web session, securing email communications, or enabling private connections between distributed systems, the Record Protocol ensures that data can be transmitted safely, reliably, and efficiently across untrusted networks. Its layered design and adaptability to modern cryptographic techniques ensure its continued relevance in a rapidly evolving digital landscape.

TLS Vulnerabilities and Mitigations

Transport Layer Security, or TLS, is a widely used protocol designed to secure communications over the internet. It provides confidentiality, integrity, and authentication through a combination of cryptographic algorithms and handshake protocols. While TLS is considered one of the most reliable ways to protect data in transit, it is not immune to vulnerabilities. Over the years, researchers and attackers have identified weaknesses in both the protocol itself and its implementations. These vulnerabilities range from theoretical cryptographic flaws to practical issues resulting from misconfiguration or outdated software. Understanding these vulnerabilities and how they are mitigated is essential for maintaining a strong and secure TLS deployment.

One of the earliest and most well-known vulnerabilities was in SSL, the predecessor of TLS. SSL 2.0 and SSL 3.0 were both found to contain critical weaknesses that made them susceptible to attacks such as POODLE, which exploited the way padding was handled in block cipher modes. The POODLE attack allowed a man-in-the-middle attacker to decrypt encrypted messages by taking advantage of fallback mechanisms and padding errors. To mitigate this, support for SSL 3.0 was deprecated, and TLS implementations were modified to disable fallback to insecure versions. Modern servers and clients are now expected to use TLS 1.2 or TLS 1.3 exclusively to avoid these legacy vulnerabilities.

TLS 1.0 and 1.1 also contain design issues that make them less secure by today's standards. These versions use outdated cryptographic primitives, including weaker cipher suites and hash functions such as MD5 and SHA-1. Additionally, they lack protection against certain types of attacks like BEAST, which exploited weaknesses in the cipher block chaining (CBC) mode. The BEAST attack allowed attackers to decrypt parts of an encrypted session by injecting specially crafted packets and analyzing the response. Mitigations for BEAST included the use of stream ciphers like RC4, but RC4 was later found to be insecure due to statistical biases. As a result, both RC4 and CBC-based cipher suites have been deprecated in favor of authenticated encryption modes like AES-GCM and ChaCha20-Poly1305, which are resistant to such attacks.

Another class of vulnerabilities affecting TLS is related to the renegotiation feature. TLS supports renegotiation of session parameters during an ongoing connection. However, early versions of the protocol did not adequately authenticate renegotiation requests, leading to the possibility of injection attacks. In a typical renegotiation attack, an attacker could insert their own commands into a secure session between a client and server, leading to unauthorized access or data leakage. To address this, a secure renegotiation extension was introduced and later became a mandatory part of updated TLS implementations.

Certificate-related vulnerabilities are also a major concern in TLS. Since TLS relies on certificate-based authentication, the security of a TLS session depends heavily on the validity and trustworthiness of digital certificates. Attacks such as certificate spoofing, misuse of wildcard certificates, and the issuance of fraudulent certificates by compromised Certificate Authorities have shown how fragile the certificate trust model can be. Notable incidents include the compromise of major CAs like DigiNotar, which led to the issuance of fake certificates for popular domains. To mitigate such threats, browsers and operating systems have implemented mechanisms like Certificate Transparency logs, strict certificate validation policies, and revocation checking via OCSP and CRLs. Certificate pinning was also introduced as a defense mechanism, although it has since fallen out of favor due to operational risks and has been replaced by more dynamic alternatives.

Downgrade attacks pose another threat to TLS security. In these attacks, a malicious actor interferes with the handshake process to force the client and server to use a less secure protocol version or cipher suite than they would normally negotiate. The FREAK and Logjam attacks are examples of downgrade attacks that exploited weak export-grade cryptography and Diffie-Hellman parameters. In response, servers are now configured to prefer strong cipher suites and disable support for known weak algorithms. Additionally, TLS 1.3 eliminated support for all known weak features and enforced mandatory protections against downgrade attempts by including version checks in the handshake transcript.

Side-channel attacks represent a more advanced category of threats against TLS. These attacks exploit timing information, cache usage, or other indirect data to infer sensitive information such as encryption keys or plaintext messages. The Lucky13 attack targeted the processing time of MAC verification in CBC mode to extract information about the plaintext. The mitigation for this attack involves implementing constant-time cryptographic operations that do not reveal information through observable timing differences. Developers of cryptographic libraries must be particularly vigilant in this regard, as even small variations in execution time can lead to exploitable leaks.

The Heartbleed vulnerability was a devastating example of an implementation flaw in a TLS library, specifically OpenSSL. It allowed attackers to read arbitrary memory from affected servers by sending specially crafted heartbeat requests. This vulnerability did not result from a problem in the TLS protocol itself but from improper bounds checking in the code. Heartbleed demonstrated the importance of rigorous code auditing, secure coding practices, and regular updates to TLS libraries. It also highlighted the potential for severe damage when cryptographic software is flawed, including the compromise of private keys and sensitive user data.

TLS session resumption features such as session tickets and 0-RTT data in TLS 1.3 introduce additional security considerations. While session resumption improves performance, it can also open the door to replay attacks or reduced forward secrecy if not implemented carefully. To address this, servers enforce strict policies on 0-RTT usage, limit resumption lifetimes, and rotate encryption keys regularly. TLS 1.3

further improves security by requiring forward secrecy even for resumed sessions, ensuring that session keys cannot be recovered even if long-term keys are compromised.

Misconfiguration remains one of the most common causes of TLS vulnerabilities in real-world deployments. Servers that support outdated protocol versions, allow weak cipher suites, or use expired or improperly signed certificates can expose users to serious risks. Tools such as security scanners and configuration analyzers help administrators identify and remediate such issues. Best practices include regularly updating TLS libraries, disabling legacy features, enforcing strong cipher suites, and automating certificate renewal using protocols like ACME.

TLS vulnerabilities, while serious, have led to continuous improvements in the protocol and its ecosystem. The cryptographic community, browser vendors, and infrastructure providers collaborate to identify weaknesses and deploy mitigations. Through the iterative development of TLS 1.0, 1.1, 1.2, and 1.3, the protocol has become increasingly resistant to both theoretical and practical attacks. Security professionals must remain vigilant, continually monitor threat developments, and ensure that their systems use the latest versions of TLS configured according to current best practices. By staying ahead of known vulnerabilities and implementing appropriate mitigations, TLS continues to provide a strong and adaptable foundation for secure communication across the internet.

TLS: Datagram Transport Layer Security

Datagram Transport Layer Security, commonly known as DTLS, is a protocol designed to provide the same level of security as Transport Layer Security (TLS) while operating over datagram-based communication protocols such as UDP instead of TCP. TLS was originally designed to function over a reliable, connection-oriented transport layer that guarantees the order and delivery of messages. However, many real-time applications, including voice over IP, online gaming, video conferencing, and some IoT systems, require low-latency, low-overhead communication and are built on top of the User

Datagram Protocol. UDP does not provide reliability or ordered delivery, which means it introduces unique challenges for implementing secure communication. DTLS was created to bridge this gap by adapting the proven security features of TLS to the more unpredictable behavior of datagram-based transport.

DTLS retains most of the core features and structure of TLS, including the record layer, handshake protocol, alert protocol, and support for cipher suites and certificates. The key difference lies in how DTLS handles issues that arise from the unreliable and unordered nature of UDP. Because UDP does not guarantee packet order or delivery, DTLS must be able to tolerate lost, reordered, or duplicated messages during the handshake and data transmission phases. This requires additional mechanisms, such as sequence numbers, timers, retransmission strategies, and fragmentation handling, to ensure that the communication remains secure even in the presence of packet loss or reordering.

The DTLS handshake is very similar to the TLS handshake, but it includes modifications to account for the lack of reliable transport. Each handshake message is assigned a sequence number, and the recipient keeps track of which messages have been received. If a message is lost or arrives out of order, the recipient can detect the gap and request retransmission. Similarly, the sender may retransmit handshake messages after a timeout if no acknowledgment is received. These retransmission strategies are carefully designed to avoid unnecessary duplication and to prevent denial-of-service attacks that could be triggered by maliciously delayed or repeated packets.

One of the challenges addressed by DTLS is the potential for denial-of-service attacks during the handshake process. Because DTLS must operate without the connection-establishment features of TCP, it is vulnerable to attacks where an attacker sends a flood of handshake initiation messages, consuming server resources and preventing legitimate clients from connecting. To mitigate this, DTLS uses a stateless cookie mechanism during the initial handshake. When the server receives a ClientHello message, it responds with a HelloVerifyRequest message that includes a cookie. The client must return this cookie in its next message, proving that it can receive and respond to data sent to its source address. Only after this validation does the server allocate memory and other resources to process the handshake, protecting it against spoofed requests.

Another critical aspect of DTLS is the preservation of data integrity and confidentiality. Like TLS, DTLS supports a wide range of cipher suites that combine symmetric encryption, message authentication, and key exchange mechanisms. These include modern and secure algorithms such as AES-GCM and ChaCha20-Poly1305, which provide authenticated encryption with associated data. DTLS also supports the use of X.509 certificates for authentication and allows for mutual authentication between client and server. The record layer of DTLS ensures that each datagram is individually secured, which means that even if packets are delivered out of order, they can still be decrypted and verified independently.

DTLS handles application data by encapsulating each message in a record that includes a sequence number, content type, length, and encryption metadata. Because UDP has a maximum transmission unit and does not support fragmentation or reassembly, DTLS must ensure that its records fit within the network's maximum datagram size. If a message is too large, it must be fragmented and each fragment sent in a separate UDP datagram. The receiving party is responsible for reassembling the fragments in the correct order. This adds complexity but is necessary to accommodate larger handshake messages or application data in environments with small MTUs.

In terms of deployment, DTLS is widely used in applications where low latency is more critical than guaranteed delivery. For instance, in voice and video applications, it is often acceptable to lose a few packets rather than introduce delays caused by retransmissions. DTLS provides encryption and authentication in these contexts without sacrificing the performance benefits of UDP. One of the most prominent uses of DTLS is in securing Web Real-Time Communication, or WebRTC, which enables peer-to-peer audio, video, and data sharing in web applications. DTLS is also used in VPN technologies such as Datagram TLS VPNs and in constrained environments through DTLS support in lightweight security protocols like CoAP for the Internet of Things.

DTLS exists in multiple versions that mirror the versions of TLS. DTLS 1.0 is based on TLS 1.1, and DTLS 1.2 is based on TLS 1.2. The latest version, DTLS 1.3, builds on the security improvements introduced in TLS 1.3, including reduced handshake complexity, mandatory forward secrecy, and the removal of obsolete cryptographic algorithms. DTLS 1.3 simplifies the handshake by reducing the number of messages and round trips needed to establish a secure session, making it even more suitable for real-time and resource-constrained applications. It also enhances resistance to known attacks and improves privacy by encrypting more handshake metadata.

Like TLS, DTLS is vulnerable to implementation flaws and must be carefully configured and maintained. Common security issues include the use of weak cipher suites, improper certificate validation, and outdated protocol versions. Developers and administrators must follow best practices, such as enforcing strong cipher suites, using short-lived session tickets, and applying patches to cryptographic libraries. The importance of secure randomness, proper key management, and constant-time cryptographic operations remains just as critical in DTLS as it is in TLS.

DTLS provides a valuable extension of TLS capabilities to applications that require fast, efficient, and secure communication over unreliable networks. By adapting the TLS model to work with UDP, it offers a robust solution for securing data in scenarios where speed and responsiveness are more important than reliability. Its widespread adoption across real-time media, mobile applications, and IoT systems underscores its importance in modern security architecture. DTLS continues to evolve alongside TLS, incorporating new cryptographic techniques and protocol enhancements that ensure it remains a trusted and effective tool for securing datagram-based communications in an increasingly connected world.

TLS vs DTLS: Key Differences

Transport Layer Security, or TLS, is the most widely used protocol for securing communication over the internet. It provides confidentiality, integrity, and authentication by encrypting data transmitted between applications and ensuring that it has not been tampered with or intercepted. Datagram Transport Layer Security, or DTLS, is a variant of TLS designed to work over datagram-based transport protocols such as UDP instead of the more reliable stream-based TCP. While DTLS and TLS share many similarities in terms of cryptographic mechanisms and overall goals, their operational differences are significant, especially in the context of the environments they are intended for. Understanding the key differences between TLS and DTLS is crucial for selecting the right protocol for a given application and ensuring optimal performance and security.

TLS is built on the assumption that it will operate over a reliable transport layer, typically TCP. This assumption allows TLS to avoid implementing its own mechanisms for handling packet loss, reordering, and duplication, as TCP already guarantees in-order delivery, retransmission of lost packets, and flow control. This reliability makes TLS suitable for applications that require a strong guarantee of message delivery and order, such as web browsing, email communication, file transfers, and secure database connections. The stability of TCP complements the design of TLS, which relies on a sequential, stateful exchange of handshake and application data.

DTLS, by contrast, is specifically engineered to provide the same level of security as TLS while operating over unreliable transport protocols like UDP. UDP does not guarantee packet delivery or order, and it allows for duplicates. Therefore, DTLS must implement additional logic within the protocol to handle these issues. For instance, DTLS introduces explicit sequence numbers to detect and discard duplicate or replayed packets. It also includes a mechanism for reordering out-of-sequence packets so that they can be processed in the correct order. These features are critical in environments where low latency and fast transmission are prioritized over absolute reliability, such as in voice-over-IP (VoIP), online gaming, and real-time video streaming.

Another key difference lies in the way each protocol handles session initiation. In TLS, the handshake process relies on the underlying TCP layer to ensure the ordered delivery of handshake messages. The client and server exchange a sequence of messages that establish the cryptographic parameters of the session, verify identities using certificates, and derive the keys used for encryption. The TCP layer handles retransmissions and ensures that each handshake message arrives intact and in order. In DTLS, this same handshake process must be adapted to account for potential packet loss or duplication. DTLS introduces a stateless cookie exchange at the beginning of the handshake, requiring the client to prove it can receive packets at its claimed address before the server allocates resources to the session. This HelloVerifyRequest mechanism helps prevent denial-of-service attacks and ensures that the handshake proceeds only when both parties are reachable.

Fragmentation is another important distinction. TLS can rely on TCP's stream-oriented model to transmit large amounts of data in a continuous flow, allowing for arbitrarily large messages to be broken up and reassembled automatically by the TCP layer. DTLS, however, must manage fragmentation internally because UDP packets are limited in size and may be dropped if they exceed the network's maximum transmission unit. DTLS fragments large handshake messages into smaller pieces and reassembles them on the receiving end. This adds complexity to the DTLS implementation but is necessary to support reliable session establishment over UDP.

Error handling and retransmission also differ significantly between the two protocols. In TLS, if a packet is lost, the TCP layer detects this and automatically resends the missing data. In DTLS, the protocol itself is responsible for detecting lost messages and initiating retransmissions. DTLS uses timers and sequence numbers to determine when a message has not been acknowledged and needs to be resent. This approach allows DTLS to operate without the overhead of TCP's congestion control mechanisms, offering faster performance in latency-sensitive applications. However, it also places more responsibility on the application and the DTLS stack to manage timeouts, retransmissions, and session state.

Security-wise, TLS and DTLS offer the same level of cryptographic protection. Both protocols use similar cipher suites, key exchange mechanisms, and certificate-based authentication. Both support modern cryptographic algorithms like AES-GCM and ChaCha20-Poly1305 and are capable of providing forward secrecy when configured with ephemeral key exchanges. The main difference is not in what security features are available but in how they are implemented given the characteristics of the underlying transport protocol. Because DTLS must function over an unreliable transport layer, it introduces additional structures such as epoch numbers and connection IDs to manage session continuity and prevent confusion between active and expired session states.

Performance is a major factor when deciding between TLS and DTLS. Applications that require guaranteed delivery, in-order data, and robustness against network instability are better suited for TLS. Applications that prioritize speed, real-time interaction, and can tolerate some degree of packet loss benefit from DTLS. For example, a secure web session transferring sensitive user information must not lose a single byte of data and can tolerate a few milliseconds of delay, making TLS over TCP the better option. In contrast, a multiplayer game where players exchange frequent updates about their position and actions cannot afford the latency introduced by retransmissions, making DTLS over UDP a more appropriate choice.

Deployment considerations also differ. TLS is deeply integrated into most web servers, browsers, and network stacks and is supported natively in almost every modern operating system. DTLS, while increasingly supported, may require additional configuration, especially for managing timeouts, handling packet fragmentation, and dealing with firewall rules that block UDP traffic. Furthermore, because UDP is more susceptible to packet loss and network filtering, applications using DTLS must be designed to cope with these realities.

Despite these differences, both TLS and DTLS continue to evolve in parallel. DTLS 1.3 is closely aligned with TLS 1.3, adopting many of its simplifications and security improvements. These include the removal of obsolete cryptographic algorithms, faster handshakes, and mandatory forward secrecy. The close alignment between the two protocols ensures that developers can apply much of their knowledge from TLS to DTLS, reducing the learning curve and encouraging broader adoption of secure UDP-based communication.

TLS and DTLS are complementary technologies, each designed to provide secure communication within the constraints of the transport protocol they support. TLS excels in scenarios where reliability and stream-oriented data are critical, while DTLS shines in applications where speed and minimal overhead are prioritized. Understanding the differences between them allows system architects and developers to make informed choices that balance performance, reliability, and security according to the needs of their specific applications. By leveraging the strengths of each protocol appropriately, organizations can ensure that their communications remain protected across a wide variety of use cases and network environments.

TLS Use Cases in Real-Time Applications

Transport Layer Security, or TLS, is a cryptographic protocol widely adopted to secure communication across diverse types of digital interactions. Although traditionally associated with securing web traffic and applications over TCP, TLS and its datagram variant, DTLS, have become increasingly relevant in the context of real-time applications. These applications require fast, low-latency, and uninterrupted communication, often over networks that are unpredictable or time-sensitive. Real-time applications are used in voice-over-IP, video conferencing, online gaming, financial trading platforms, instant messaging, and remote control systems, where milliseconds of delay or a short disruption in data transmission can significantly impact performance and user experience. The challenge lies in applying strong encryption and authentication mechanisms without introducing prohibitive overhead, and this is where TLS and DTLS prove their value.

In real-time voice and video applications, such as VoIP calls and video conferencing tools like Zoom, Google Meet, and Microsoft Teams, maintaining privacy and data integrity is essential. These applications often rely on UDP to achieve low latency, since it allows data to be sent without waiting for acknowledgments or retransmissions. TLS in its traditional form is not designed for such communication, as it depends on the reliable, ordered delivery provided by TCP. However, DTLS offers a solution that brings the full strength of TLS cryptographic protection to UDP-based protocols. DTLS ensures that media streams remain encrypted from end to end, preventing unauthorized interception while allowing packets to flow efficiently, even in lossy or congested network conditions.

WebRTC, a standard that enables real-time communication directly between browsers, heavily relies on DTLS for securing its media and data channels. In WebRTC, DTLS is used during the peer connection process to establish secure encryption keys, which are then used to protect audio, video, and other forms of media. This approach avoids the need for proprietary encryption layers and ensures interoperability across platforms and devices. The use of DTLS in WebRTC also supports features such as perfect forward secrecy and mutual authentication, making it one of the most robust security architectures available for browser-based communication. Since WebRTC is widely used in telemedicine, online education, and virtual events, the secure transmission of sensitive personal and medical information is critical.

In the realm of online gaming, real-time responsiveness is key to delivering a smooth and competitive user experience. Multiplayer games often exchange hundreds of messages per second, including position updates, player actions, and environmental changes. Using TLS over TCP in these scenarios can lead to undesirable delays due to packet retransmission and congestion control. Instead, many games use DTLS over UDP to maintain encrypted communication channels without sacrificing speed. While some level of packet loss is tolerated in gaming, the integrity and authenticity of data packets must still be ensured to prevent cheating or tampering. DTLS allows game servers and clients to verify the origin of messages and confirm that they have not been altered, while keeping latency to a minimum.

Instant messaging and chat applications also benefit from TLS when real-time message delivery is required. These applications typically involve the exchange of small packets of data that must be delivered quickly and securely. TLS is used not only for securing the initial login and session setup but also for ensuring that every message sent between users is encrypted and authenticated. Protocols like XMPP and Matrix implement TLS to protect message delivery over TCP, maintaining confidentiality and resistance to interception. For mobile messaging platforms that need to resume communication quickly after brief network interruptions, TLS session resumption mechanisms help reduce the time and computational cost associated with re-establishing secure connections.

Real-time financial applications, such as electronic trading systems and payment processing platforms, demand extremely low latency combined with the highest level of security. These systems are often built using specialized messaging protocols that must support real-time market data, order placement, and transaction verification. TLS is employed to protect these interactions, ensuring that orders and financial data cannot be modified or observed in transit. In some cases, DTLS is used to protect lightweight messaging over UDP in latency-sensitive environments. Given the potential consequences of data breaches or manipulation in financial systems, robust certificate-based authentication and mutual TLS are often implemented to verify both client and server identities before any sensitive data is exchanged.

Remote control systems and industrial automation networks increasingly rely on secure communication channels as part of the broader adoption of Industry 4.0 technologies. Whether it's a factory robot being controlled remotely, a drone receiving flight instructions, or a medical device transmitting patient data, real-time interaction and encryption are both essential. TLS and DTLS provide the foundation for secure machine-to-machine communication, allowing commands to be delivered without delay and ensuring that responses are authenticated. The lightweight nature of DTLS makes it especially attractive in constrained environments where bandwidth and processing power are limited.

TLS is also used in live streaming platforms, where the need for high-throughput and low-latency video transmission must be balanced against the requirement for content protection. While media content is often delivered via protocols like HTTP Live Streaming (HLS) or MPEG-DASH over TCP, TLS is employed to encrypt these streams from the source server to the end user. For real-time interactive streaming, such as in live auctions or interactive sports broadcasts, DTLS may be integrated with RTP-based protocols to enable faster and more direct transmission of media while preserving encryption and integrity.

Furthermore, TLS plays a significant role in real-time control applications in critical infrastructure, such as energy grids, transportation systems, and emergency response networks. These systems often rely on SCADA protocols and IoT frameworks that historically lacked strong security. With the increased risk of cyberattacks on infrastructure, TLS and DTLS have been integrated into new standards and protocols to provide encryption and authentication for control messages and telemetry data. This ensures that real-time monitoring and control functions are protected against tampering, spoofing, and interception.

The adoption of TLS in real-time applications is not without challenges. Implementers must carefully balance security, performance, and reliability. Choosing between TLS and DTLS often depends on the specific requirements of the application, the nature of the network environment, and the acceptable level of data loss or latency. Developers must also pay close attention to secure configuration, including proper certificate management, cipher suite selection, and session handling. Misconfigurations can expose real-time systems to vulnerabilities, such as weak encryption or unauthorized access, undermining the benefits of using TLS in the first place.

Despite these challenges, TLS and DTLS have proven to be adaptable and resilient technologies capable of meeting the demands of modern real-time communication. Their use across a wide range of applications demonstrates how foundational secure communication has become in our daily digital interactions. Whether enabling a secure voice call, protecting game data, ensuring financial transactions, or safeguarding critical infrastructure, TLS continues to be a cornerstone of real-time security in an increasingly connected world.

TLS Handshake and Record Protocols

The Transport Layer Security protocol, known as TLS, is designed to provide secure communication over a network. It achieves this goal through a combination of two core protocols: the TLS Handshake Protocol and the TLS Record Protocol. These two work together in every secure session, ensuring that information exchanged between a client and server remains private, authenticated, and tamper-proof. While they operate in distinct ways, both are essential to the successful establishment and maintenance of a TLS connection.

The TLS Handshake Protocol is responsible for the initial negotiation between the client and the server. It allows both parties to agree on cryptographic parameters, verify each other's identities, and establish shared secrets for encryption and authentication. The handshake begins when the client sends a message called ClientHello to the server. This message includes a range of information, such as the highest TLS version the client supports, a list of supported cipher suites, random values used for key generation, and any optional extensions. The server replies with a ServerHello message, choosing the TLS version, selecting a compatible cipher suite, providing its own random value, and often presenting a digital certificate used to authenticate its identity.

During this process, public key cryptography is used to exchange key material securely. The exact method depends on the cipher suite chosen. In older versions of TLS, this often involved the client generating a pre-master secret and encrypting it with the server's public key. More modern versions, including TLS 1.2 and especially TLS 1.3, rely on ephemeral Diffie-Hellman or Elliptic Curve Diffie-Hellman methods to establish a shared key without ever directly transmitting it. These methods enable forward secrecy, ensuring that even if long-term keys are compromised in the future, past communication cannot be decrypted.

In addition to negotiating cryptographic parameters, the handshake includes mutual authentication steps. While the server typically presents a certificate signed by a trusted Certificate Authority, some configurations require the client to also present a certificate. This form of mutual TLS provides strong two-way authentication and is especially important in environments such as enterprise networks, banking systems, or secure APIs. After the server's certificate is received, the client verifies its authenticity, expiration date, and whether it was issued by a trusted authority.

Once key exchange is complete and authentication is verified, both client and server generate session keys from the shared secret and the random values exchanged earlier. They then exchange Finished messages, which are encrypted and contain hashes of all the handshake messages sent so far. This ensures that the entire handshake has not been tampered with. If the hashes match, both parties confirm that they are synchronized and can now proceed to secure communication using the negotiated session keys.

The TLS Record Protocol is the layer responsible for encapsulating and securing actual application data. Once the handshake is complete and session keys have been established, all data exchanged between the client and the server is handled by the Record Protocol. It takes data from the application layer, breaks it into manageable blocks, and secures each block before transmitting it across the network. Each TLS record includes a header specifying the type of data being sent, the version of the protocol, and the length of the payload. After this header, the actual data follows, typically encrypted and authenticated.

The Record Protocol supports multiple content types, including application data, handshake messages, alerts, and change cipher spec messages. Regardless of the content type, the Record Protocol applies the same general process to all records. First, it may compress the data, though compression is rarely used in modern versions due to vulnerabilities like CRIME. Next, it applies a Message Authentication Code if using a cipher suite that separates encryption and authentication. Finally, it encrypts the entire block using the negotiated cipher and session keys. Modern cipher suites use authenticated encryption methods like AES-GCM or ChaCha20-Poly1305, which combine encryption and integrity checks in a single step.

On the receiving side, the Record Protocol reverses the process. It decrypts the received data using the appropriate session key, verifies the message's authenticity, decompresses if necessary, and delivers the plaintext to the application layer. If any part of this process fails—if the message fails authentication, if the data is corrupted, or if the record is malformed—the protocol discards the data and may terminate the session. This strict behavior ensures that attackers cannot inject or modify data without being detected.

TLS also includes sequence numbers as part of its Record Protocol processing, although these are not transmitted over the network. Each side of the connection maintains its own sequence number, which increments with each record. This number is included in the MAC calculation or the authenticated encryption operation, preventing attackers from reordering or replaying messages. Sequence numbers also help identify lost records and protect the session from subtle attacks that could otherwise go undetected.

Throughout the life of a TLS session, the Record Protocol provides confidentiality and integrity, while the Handshake Protocol ensures that the initial security parameters were properly negotiated and verified. Together, they form a tightly integrated security architecture that has evolved over time. TLS 1.3 brought significant simplifications to both protocols, streamlining the handshake to complete in fewer round trips and removing support for outdated cipher suites and key exchange methods. It also encrypted more of the handshake messages, improving privacy and reducing the potential for metadata leakage.

TLS sessions can be resumed using abbreviated handshakes, allowing the client and server to reuse previously established session parameters. This improves performance, especially in environments with frequent reconnects or limited resources. The Record Protocol continues to secure data even in resumed sessions, using newly derived session keys for each connection. Security is maintained without repeating the full handshake, reducing latency and CPU usage.

Alerts are another function of TLS handled by the Record Protocol. These are special messages that notify the peer of errors, warnings, or session termination. They are critical for maintaining the integrity of the session and for signaling when something has gone wrong. Common alerts include unexpected messages, decryption failures, and certificate validation issues. These alerts are also encrypted and authenticated, ensuring they are not spoofed or modified in transit.

The architecture of TLS, through its Handshake and Record Protocols, provides a flexible and powerful framework for securing digital communication. It balances the need for strong cryptography, performance, and reliability, making it suitable for a wide range of applications and network environments. From the moment a connection is initiated to the final byte of data transmitted, these two protocols work in tandem to ensure that communication remains private, authenticated, and trustworthy. This design has enabled TLS to become the backbone of internet security and a critical component of digital trust in the modern world.

Securing VoIP and Media with SRTP

Voice over IP, or VoIP, has become the dominant method of voice communication in both enterprise and consumer environments. It replaces traditional circuit-switched telephone systems with packet-switched data networks, allowing voice and video calls to be transmitted over the internet or private IP networks. While VoIP offers cost savings, scalability, and integration with other digital services, it also introduces new security challenges. Voice, video, and other real-time media streams are transmitted in formats that can be intercepted, tampered with, or replayed if not adequately protected. To address these risks, the Secure Real-time Transport Protocol, or SRTP, was developed to provide confidentiality, message authentication, and integrity for RTP-based media streams without introducing excessive latency or complexity.

SRTP is an extension of the Real-time Transport Protocol, RTP, which is widely used to carry audio and video traffic in real-time applications such as VoIP calls, video conferencing, and streaming media. RTP, by itself, provides no security. It was designed to deliver media with precise timing and minimal delay, but its headers and payloads are transmitted in plaintext, making it vulnerable to eavesdropping and manipulation. SRTP adds a layer of cryptographic protection to RTP while preserving its real-time characteristics. It encrypts the media payload to keep conversations private, applies message authentication codes to verify integrity and origin, and supports replay protection to block malicious reuse of previously captured packets.

The core strength of SRTP lies in its ability to secure media streams without disrupting the timing-sensitive nature of real-time communication. Unlike traditional encryption protocols that may introduce delays due to handshake procedures or retransmission logic, SRTP is designed to be lightweight and fast. It operates at the application layer, directly securing the RTP packets that carry voice and video data. This allows it to be implemented efficiently in software or hardware, including in IP phones, media gateways, and mobile devices. By avoiding heavy cryptographic operations or complex session management, SRTP ensures that security does not come at the expense of performance.

Encryption in SRTP is applied only to the payload of RTP packets, leaving the RTP header untouched. This decision allows intermediate network devices, such as routers, switches, and quality-of-service engines, to inspect and manage RTP flows based on header information like sequence numbers, timestamps, and payload types. This visibility is essential for maintaining low latency and high quality of service, especially in large-scale deployments or congested network environments. SRTP supports multiple encryption algorithms, with the Advanced Encryption Standard, AES, being the default. It uses AES in counter mode (AES-CTR) for encryption and AES-based message authentication codes (AES-CMAC or HMAC-SHA1) for integrity and authentication.

Key management is a critical component of SRTP. While SRTP itself focuses on the protection of media packets, it does not define how cryptographic keys are generated or exchanged. Instead, it relies on external key management protocols to provide keys in a secure and timely manner. The most common methods used are DTLS-SRTP and SDES. DTLS-SRTP uses Datagram Transport Layer Security to perform a secure handshake and negotiate key material between the communicating parties. It is widely adopted in modern systems and is part of the WebRTC standard, providing secure media for browser-based voice and video calls. SDES, or the Session Description Protocol Security Descriptions, transmits keys out-of-band within SIP signaling messages. While easier to implement, SDES is less secure than DTLS-SRTP because it exposes key material to potential interception unless the signaling path is also encrypted using protocols like TLS.

Replay protection is another vital feature of SRTP. Because RTP packets are transmitted over unreliable networks such as the internet, they may be captured and retransmitted by attackers in an attempt to confuse or disrupt communication. SRTP uses sequence numbers and a sliding window mechanism to detect and reject replayed packets. Each packet is tagged with a sequence number, and the receiver maintains a record of recently received packets. If a duplicate is detected or if a packet arrives outside the expected range, it is discarded. This protects against a variety of denial-of-service and impersonation attacks that could otherwise compromise the integrity of a call.

SRTP also supports optional encryption of RTP header extensions, which may contain sensitive metadata about a session or user. While these headers are not encrypted by default, enabling their encryption can provide additional privacy for systems that use advanced features like audio level indicators, synchronization data, or user identification tokens. Protecting this information is especially important in applications like telehealth, secure conferencing, or government communications, where metadata leaks could reveal patterns of behavior or associations between individuals.

The deployment of SRTP is now considered best practice for any VoIP or real-time media system. Organizations that handle sensitive voice or video data—such as financial institutions, healthcare providers, law firms, and government agencies—often mandate SRTP as part of their regulatory compliance and risk mitigation strategies. Even in consumer applications, users increasingly expect encrypted communication as a standard feature. Services like Skype, Zoom, and WhatsApp use variations of SRTP to provide end-to-end encryption for their voice and video calls, helping to build trust and confidence in the platform.

Despite its advantages, SRTP must be correctly configured and integrated into the overall communication architecture. Poor key management, outdated cipher suites, or incorrect implementation can weaken security or lead to interoperability issues. For example, if one endpoint supports only SDES and the other supports only DTLS-SRTP, the call may fail to establish a secure media session. Administrators must ensure that all devices in the communication path are SRTP-capable and that key exchange methods are compatible. Logging, monitoring, and regular updates are also necessary to maintain the security posture of SRTP-enabled systems.

SRTP has also been extended to support secure transmission of feedback messages through SRTCP, or Secure Real-time Transport Control Protocol. SRTCP secures control messages such as quality reports, synchronization information, and session termination signals. These messages, while not containing media content, are critical to the operation of the session and can be used by attackers to interfere with or monitor call quality if left unprotected. By securing both RTP and

RTCP traffic, SRTP provides a comprehensive framework for protecting all aspects of a real-time communication session.

In modern communication systems, securing real-time media is no longer optional. As threats become more sophisticated and as privacy expectations rise, protocols like SRTP serve a crucial role in ensuring that voice and video data remain confidential, trustworthy, and uninterrupted. By encrypting the payload, authenticating packets, and enabling flexible key management, SRTP empowers developers, providers, and users to engage in secure conversations across any network, from private enterprise systems to global internet platforms. Its design balances the demands of real-time performance with the requirements of strong security, making it a cornerstone technology in today's rapidly evolving digital communication landscape.

Secure Shell (SSH) Protocol

The Secure Shell protocol, commonly known as SSH, is a cryptographic network protocol used to establish secure and authenticated communication between two systems over an insecure network. It was created to replace older, less secure protocols like Telnet, rlogin, and FTP, which transmitted data, including passwords, in plaintext, making them highly susceptible to eavesdropping and other attacks. SSH solves this problem by encrypting the entire session, ensuring that all data exchanged between the client and the server is protected from unauthorized access, interception, and tampering. Since its introduction in the mid-1990s, SSH has become a standard tool for system administrators, developers, and network engineers, enabling remote management, file transfer, and secure tunneling.

At its core, SSH operates on a client-server model. The client initiates a connection to the server, which then responds by presenting its public key as part of the authentication and key exchange process. The client validates the server's identity, and the two parties establish an encrypted session through a secure handshake. This handshake includes negotiation of encryption algorithms, message authentication codes, and key exchange methods. The result is a secure channel through which both command execution and data transfer can occur without exposure to threats like man-in-the-middle attacks or packet sniffing.

The SSH protocol consists of three main layers: the transport layer, the user authentication layer, and the connection layer. The transport layer is responsible for providing confidentiality, integrity, and server authentication. It establishes the encrypted session and ensures that all transmitted packets are protected using symmetric encryption algorithms, such as AES or ChaCha20, and verified using message authentication codes. The key exchange process at this layer can use various algorithms, including Diffie-Hellman, Elliptic Curve Diffie-Hellman, or RSA, depending on the configuration and the capabilities of the client and server.

The user authentication layer follows the transport layer and is responsible for authenticating the identity of the client. SSH supports multiple authentication methods, including password-based authentication, public key authentication, and more advanced techniques such as Kerberos or two-factor authentication. Among these, public key authentication is considered the most secure and scalable. In this method, the client presents a cryptographic signature generated using its private key, which the server verifies using the corresponding public key stored in the user's account. This approach eliminates the need to transmit passwords over the network and reduces the risk of brute force or dictionary attacks.

The connection layer sits on top of the authenticated and encrypted session and is responsible for managing multiple logical channels within a single SSH connection. These channels can be used for various purposes, such as executing remote commands, starting interactive shell sessions, or transferring files. One of the powerful features of SSH is its ability to multiplex multiple sessions over a single connection, enabling simultaneous command execution, port forwarding, and file transfer without opening multiple sockets or connections. This layer also supports flow control, session requests, and channel closing operations, ensuring that resources are properly managed and released when no longer needed.

One of the most widely used features of SSH is remote command execution. By initiating an SSH session, users can log into remote systems and run commands as if they were sitting at a local terminal. This capability is essential for remote system administration, allowing administrators to perform updates, monitor performance, troubleshoot issues, and automate tasks across distributed environments. SSH sessions can be scripted and managed using automation tools, enabling efficient management of large-scale infrastructures and cloud-based deployments.

In addition to remote access, SSH supports secure file transfer through protocols such as SCP and SFTP. SCP, or Secure Copy Protocol, is a simple and fast method for copying files between systems, while SFTP, or SSH File Transfer Protocol, offers a more comprehensive solution with features like directory listing, file removal, and permission changes. Both protocols leverage the SSH transport layer to ensure that file contents and metadata are encrypted and protected during transit. These tools are commonly used for backups, configuration management, and secure data distribution across networks.

SSH also provides robust port forwarding capabilities, which allow users to create encrypted tunnels for other network services. This feature, also known as SSH tunneling, can be used to securely access internal systems, bypass firewalls, or encrypt otherwise insecure protocols. There are three types of port forwarding supported by SSH: local, remote, and dynamic. Local port forwarding allows a client to forward traffic from a local port to a remote destination. Remote port forwarding enables the server to forward traffic from a port on the server to the client or another system. Dynamic port forwarding functions like a SOCKS proxy, allowing flexible and dynamic routing of traffic through the SSH tunnel. These capabilities are particularly useful in secure remote access scenarios, development environments, and network troubleshooting.

Security in SSH is further enhanced by host key verification. When a client connects to a server for the first time, the server presents its public host key. The client can store this key locally and verify it on subsequent connections to prevent impersonation attacks. If the server's key changes unexpectedly, the client is warned, indicating a possible security breach. This mechanism helps protect against man-in-the-middle attacks by ensuring that the client is always connecting to the correct and trusted server.

SSH configurations are highly customizable, allowing administrators to enforce strict security policies, control access to specific users, and limit command execution through tools like forced commands and restricted shells. Features such as key-based authentication with passphrases, idle session timeouts, IP whitelisting, and logging help further secure SSH deployments. Additionally, tools like ssh-agent and ssh-add help manage private keys securely, making it easier for users to authenticate without repeatedly entering their passphrases.

Despite its strengths, SSH must be deployed carefully to avoid misconfigurations that could compromise security. Weak passwords, exposed private keys, or outdated software versions can leave systems vulnerable to attack. Regular audits, key rotation, and adherence to best practices are essential for maintaining a secure SSH environment. The use of tools like Fail2ban can help block IP addresses after repeated failed login attempts, reducing the risk of brute-force attacks.

SSH has evolved significantly over the years, with open-source implementations like OpenSSH leading the way in both functionality and adoption. It is now a foundational technology in secure system administration, cloud computing, DevOps practices, and even automated configuration management. Its versatility, strong cryptographic foundations, and ability to adapt to a wide range of use cases have made SSH indispensable in modern computing environments. Whether used for interactive logins, automated scripts, secure data transfers, or encrypted tunnels, SSH continues to provide a trusted, efficient, and secure channel for managing and communicating across networked systems.

Secure Email Protocols: S/MIME and PGP

Email remains one of the most widely used forms of digital communication, essential for both personal and professional interactions. Despite its ubiquity, standard email protocols were not designed with security in mind. Messages are often transmitted in plaintext, making them vulnerable to interception, spoofing, tampering, and unauthorized access. To mitigate these risks and provide confidentiality, integrity, and authenticity in email communication, secure email protocols such as S/MIME and PGP were developed. Both protocols apply strong cryptographic techniques to protect email messages, but they differ in architecture, key management, and usage. Understanding how S/MIME and PGP operate is essential for anyone seeking to secure their email communications effectively.

S/MIME, or Secure/Multipurpose Internet Mail Extensions, is a standard developed to enable end-to-end encryption and digital signing of email messages. It integrates seamlessly with existing email infrastructure and leverages the X.509 public key infrastructure for certificate-based authentication. When a user sends an S/MIME-encrypted email, the message content is encrypted using a symmetric encryption algorithm such as AES, and the symmetric key is then encrypted using the recipient's public key, which is extracted from their digital certificate. This two-layer approach ensures that only the intended recipient, who possesses the corresponding private key, can decrypt the message content.

Digital signatures in S/MIME serve to verify the identity of the sender and ensure that the message has not been altered in transit. When a message is signed, the sender's email client creates a cryptographic hash of the message content and encrypts that hash with the sender's private key. The recipient's client then decrypts the hash using the sender's public key and compares it with a freshly calculated hash of the received message. If the two hashes match, the message is verified as authentic and untampered. This mechanism not only confirms the origin of the message but also protects against email spoofing and phishing attempts.

The use of X.509 certificates in S/MIME introduces a hierarchical trust model, in which a Certificate Authority, or CA, issues digital certificates to users. These certificates are signed by the CA and can be validated by other users who trust the CA. This model simplifies trust management in corporate environments where centralized control over user identities is beneficial. Enterprises often deploy their own internal certificate authorities to issue S/MIME certificates to employees, ensuring that secure email practices are maintained across the organization.

While S/MIME is powerful and widely supported by enterprise-grade email clients like Microsoft Outlook and Apple Mail, it has limitations. Key management and distribution can be complex, especially outside controlled environments. Obtaining and renewing digital certificates may involve cost and administrative overhead. Moreover, interoperability between clients can sometimes be inconsistent, particularly when dealing with attachments, formatting, or multiple recipients.

PGP, or Pretty Good Privacy, was developed as a decentralized alternative to S/MIME. Unlike S/MIME, which relies on a hierarchical certificate authority model, PGP uses a web of trust. In this system, users generate their own key pairs and can independently sign the keys of others to vouch for their authenticity. Trust is established through personal knowledge, mutual acquaintances, or key-signing events, rather than relying on a central authority. This model empowers users to control their own identity and trust relationships but requires a greater level of technical understanding and user involvement.

Encryption with PGP is conceptually similar to S/MIME. The email message is encrypted using a symmetric algorithm, and the symmetric key is then encrypted with the recipient's public key. PGP supports a variety of encryption and hash algorithms, including RSA, ElGamal, AES, and SHA-2. When a user receives a PGP-encrypted message, their private key is used to decrypt the symmetric key, which is then used to decrypt the message content. PGP signatures work by hashing the message and encrypting the hash with the sender's private key, allowing recipients to verify the integrity and origin of the message.

One of PGP's strengths is its flexibility and platform independence. It is available as both commercial and open-source implementations, such as GnuPG. PGP can be used through command-line tools, standalone applications, or plugins that integrate with email clients. However, the decentralized nature of PGP also poses challenges. Users must manage their own keys securely, back them up, and distribute their public keys to intended correspondents. If a user loses their private key, they permanently lose access to their encrypted messages. If their private key is compromised, past encrypted messages can be decrypted unless forward secrecy is applied.

The web of trust model can become difficult to scale in large or loosely connected communities. Determining which keys are trustworthy and maintaining key validity over time requires ongoing effort. Despite these challenges, PGP remains popular among privacy-conscious users, activists, journalists, and security professionals. Its open architecture and lack of dependence on central authorities appeal to those who value autonomy and control over their digital communications.

Both S/MIME and PGP offer effective solutions for securing email, but their adoption varies across different environments. S/MIME is favored in corporate settings where centralized control, policy enforcement, and integration with directory services like LDAP or Active Directory are essential. PGP, on the other hand, is often adopted by individuals and smaller groups who prefer a peer-to-peer trust model. In some cases, users employ both systems, depending on the context and recipient.

Recent developments in secure email protocols aim to simplify key management and improve user experience. Projects like Autocrypt and OpenPGP.js seek to make PGP easier to use by automating key exchange and configuration. Similarly, integration of S/MIME support into mobile devices and webmail platforms continues to expand. Despite these improvements, secure email remains a niche practice compared to the widespread use of standard, unsecured email protocols. This is partly due to usability barriers, limited awareness, and the inconvenience of managing encryption keys.

Nevertheless, in a world where data breaches, surveillance, and privacy violations are increasingly common, the importance of securing email cannot be overstated. Whether through S/MIME's enterprise-ready certificate infrastructure or PGP's decentralized model, both protocols offer robust and mature solutions to protect sensitive communication. Users who adopt secure email practices take a significant step toward reclaiming privacy, resisting unauthorized surveillance, and ensuring the authenticity of their digital interactions. With thoughtful implementation, regular training, and strong organizational support, S/MIME and PGP can form the backbone of a secure communication strategy for individuals and institutions alike.

HTTPS: HTTP over TLS

HTTPS, or Hypertext Transfer Protocol Secure, is the secure version of the standard HTTP protocol used for communication on the World Wide Web. It combines HTTP with the Transport Layer Security protocol to provide encryption, integrity, and authentication for data exchanged between a client, typically a web browser, and a server. While HTTP alone transmits data in plaintext, making it susceptible to interception and tampering, HTTPS ensures that every bit of information, including login credentials, payment details, and personal messages, is encrypted and protected from unauthorized access. As the internet has evolved into a platform for banking, commerce, communication, and critical infrastructure, HTTPS has become a foundational technology for protecting digital privacy and trust.

When a user visits a website using HTTPS, the browser and the server engage in a TLS handshake before any HTTP data is exchanged. This handshake negotiates cryptographic parameters such as the TLS version, cipher suites, and key exchange method. The server presents its digital certificate, which contains its public key and is signed by a trusted Certificate Authority. The client verifies this certificate against its list of trusted CAs, confirming the server's identity and ensuring that the user is connecting to the intended website. Once the handshake is complete and a shared session key is established, the browser and server use symmetric encryption to protect all subsequent HTTP messages.

The use of symmetric encryption ensures that data transmitted over HTTPS cannot be read or modified by attackers who intercept the traffic. This is essential in preventing eavesdropping and man-in-the-middle attacks, where malicious actors position themselves between the client and server to steal or manipulate data. Additionally, HTTPS provides message authentication, ensuring that any tampering with data in transit is detected immediately. This integrity protection is crucial in maintaining the trustworthiness of web content, particularly in sensitive transactions such as online banking, e-commerce, and government communications.

HTTPS also supports features such as forward secrecy, which ensures that the compromise of long-term keys does not affect the confidentiality of past sessions. This is achieved through the use of ephemeral key exchanges, such as those based on Diffie-Hellman or Elliptic Curve Diffie-Hellman algorithms. With forward secrecy, even if an attacker gains access to the server's private key at a later time, previously recorded encrypted sessions remain secure and unreadable. This makes HTTPS especially resilient in environments where data confidentiality must be preserved over long periods.

The importance of HTTPS has grown alongside the rise of threats such as phishing, data breaches, and surveillance. Modern web browsers now mark HTTP sites as "Not Secure," especially when users are asked to input sensitive information. Search engines also factor HTTPS into their ranking algorithms, encouraging widespread adoption of the protocol. Websites without HTTPS are at a disadvantage in terms of both security and visibility. This has led to a significant shift in web development practices, where HTTPS is considered a default requirement for any public-facing site.

The process of enabling HTTPS on a website involves obtaining a digital certificate, configuring the web server, and enforcing secure communication. Traditionally, acquiring a certificate required payment and manual verification through a Certificate Authority. However, initiatives such as Let's Encrypt have made it possible to obtain certificates for free through an automated protocol called ACME. Let's Encrypt and similar services have significantly lowered the barrier to entry, allowing even small websites and individual developers to deploy HTTPS easily. Automation tools such as Certbot simplify the process of installing, renewing, and managing certificates, further accelerating adoption.

Beyond basic encryption, HTTPS supports a range of features that enhance web security. HTTP Strict Transport Security, or HSTS, is a response header that tells browsers to only access a site over HTTPS, even if the user attempts to visit the HTTP version. This prevents downgrade attacks, where an attacker tries to force a client to fall back to an insecure HTTP connection. Similarly, certificate pinning was once used to associate a site with a specific certificate or public key, although it has been largely replaced by Certificate Transparency and other modern mechanisms due to deployment challenges.

HTTPS is also integral to modern web application performance through its support of newer protocols like HTTP/2 and HTTP/3. These protocols require HTTPS to function and offer substantial performance benefits, including multiplexed connections, header compression, and reduced latency. HTTP/3, in particular, is built on top of the QUIC transport protocol, which uses UDP instead of TCP and includes TLS 1.3 by default. This integration further demonstrates the growing connection between web performance and security, where the use of HTTPS not only protects users but also improves user experience through faster page loads and reduced connection overhead.

Mobile applications, APIs, and Internet of Things devices also rely on HTTPS to secure communication with servers and cloud platforms. In these contexts, HTTPS ensures that sensitive data, such as personal health information, financial transactions, or remote control commands, are not exposed or manipulated. Developers must implement HTTPS correctly, including verifying certificates and handling errors securely, to avoid introducing vulnerabilities. Poor implementation can lead to issues such as certificate validation bypass, which attackers can exploit to intercept or alter communications.

Despite its strengths, HTTPS is not a complete solution to all web security problems. It protects data in transit but does not address issues such as malicious content on the server, client-side vulnerabilities like cross-site scripting, or weak user passwords. Therefore, HTTPS should be considered one layer of a broader security strategy that includes secure coding practices, regular updates, intrusion detection, and user education. Still, without HTTPS, any sensitive data transmitted over the internet is fundamentally insecure.

The visibility of HTTPS to end users, indicated by the lock icon in browsers, plays a key role in user trust. However, this visual indicator can sometimes be misleading, as even phishing websites can obtain HTTPS certificates. Users must understand that the presence of HTTPS means that the connection is secure, but it does not guarantee the legitimacy of the website itself. Educating users on how to interpret HTTPS indicators, verify domain names, and recognize fraudulent sites remains a critical aspect of online safety.

As digital communication continues to expand, the role of HTTPS grows more central in ensuring that web interactions remain confidential and reliable. From simple browsing to complex transactions, HTTPS is the standard that underpins secure web communication. Its implementation protects users, builds trust, and forms the foundation upon which secure digital experiences are built. As adoption becomes near-universal and browsers enforce stricter standards, HTTPS represents not just a technical upgrade but a fundamental shift in how the internet approaches privacy and data protection.

VPN Technologies and Protocols

Virtual Private Network, or VPN, technologies have become essential tools for ensuring secure communication over public and untrusted networks. A VPN creates a private, encrypted tunnel between a user's device and a remote server, enabling the safe transmission of data and shielding it from potential threats like eavesdropping, data manipulation, or traffic analysis. VPNs are widely used by businesses to allow remote employees to access internal resources, by individuals to protect their online privacy, and by organizations to securely connect different network segments or remote offices. Over the years, a variety of VPN technologies and protocols have emerged, each offering specific features, advantages, and trade-offs. Understanding how these technologies work is key to selecting the most appropriate solution for different use cases and environments.

At the heart of any VPN system is the concept of tunneling. Tunneling refers to the process of encapsulating one network protocol within another, allowing private network traffic to be securely routed through a public infrastructure like the internet. This encapsulated traffic is then encrypted to ensure confidentiality and authenticated to protect against tampering. The tunnel also supports routing and addressing, enabling remote users or devices to appear as if they are part of the internal network. VPN protocols vary primarily in how they implement tunneling, encryption, and authentication, as well as in their performance and compatibility.

One of the earliest and most widely adopted VPN protocols is Point-to-Point Tunneling Protocol, or PPTP. It was developed by a consortium led by Microsoft and became popular due to its simplicity and native support in many operating systems. PPTP establishes tunnels using the Generic Routing Encapsulation protocol and authenticates users via the Point-to-Point Protocol. However, PPTP has significant security vulnerabilities, including weak encryption algorithms and susceptibility to brute-force attacks. While it offers fast performance due to minimal overhead, it is no longer considered secure and is not recommended for any scenario where confidentiality and integrity are required.

A more robust and secure option is Layer 2 Tunneling Protocol, or L2TP, typically combined with IPsec to provide encryption. L2TP on its own does not offer encryption, but when paired with IPsec, it forms a secure and versatile VPN solution. L2TP/IPsec tunnels encapsulate data twice: once using L2TP and again using IPsec, which adds security but also increases overhead and may impact performance. The protocol is widely supported across platforms and provides strong encryption, typically using AES or 3DES. It also supports a variety of authentication methods and is generally more resilient against attacks than PPTP. L2TP/IPsec is often used in enterprise environments where compatibility with legacy systems is necessary.

Another widely used VPN protocol is OpenVPN, which is open-source, highly configurable, and known for its strong security features. OpenVPN operates at the transport layer and uses the OpenSSL library to support a range of cryptographic algorithms, including AES, Blowfish, and RSA. It can operate over either UDP or TCP, allowing it to adapt to different network conditions and firewall restrictions. OpenVPN uses SSL/TLS for key exchange, providing features like mutual authentication, perfect forward secrecy, and certificate-based access control. Its open-source nature has led to widespread scrutiny and trust within the security community, and it remains a popular choice for both commercial and personal VPN services. OpenVPN is often deployed with advanced features such as load balancing, high availability, and client configuration management.

IPsec, short for Internet Protocol Security, is a protocol suite used to secure IP communications by authenticating and encrypting each IP packet in a session. Unlike other VPN protocols that operate at higher layers, IPsec functions at the network layer, allowing it to protect any application traffic without modification. It supports two modes: transport mode, which encrypts only the payload of the IP packet, and tunnel mode, which encrypts the entire packet and adds a new IP header. Tunnel mode is typically used in site-to-site VPNs connecting entire networks. IPsec relies on protocols such as IKE and IKEv2 to negotiate security associations and manage key exchange. Its flexibility and integration into modern operating systems make it a preferred choice for enterprise and governmental deployments.

WireGuard is a newer VPN protocol that has gained rapid popularity due to its simplicity, speed, and modern cryptographic design. It was developed to address the complexity and performance limitations of older VPN protocols. WireGuard uses state-of-the-art cryptographic primitives such as ChaCha20 for encryption, Poly1305 for authentication, and Curve25519 for key exchange. It operates at the network layer and is implemented as a kernel module for maximum performance. One of WireGuard's distinguishing features is its minimal codebase, which enhances security by reducing the attack surface and making auditing easier. Despite its relatively recent emergence, WireGuard has been integrated into major operating systems including Linux, Windows, macOS, and mobile platforms. It is particularly well-suited for mobile devices and modern applications requiring high-speed, low-latency connectivity.

Secure Socket Tunneling Protocol, or SSTP, is another VPN protocol developed by Microsoft. It encapsulates PPP traffic over an SSL/TLS channel, using port 443 to easily bypass firewalls and NAT devices. SSTP provides strong encryption and is tightly integrated with Windows, making it a convenient option for environments based on Microsoft technologies. However, its proprietary nature and limited support outside the Windows ecosystem have restricted its adoption in broader contexts. Still, SSTP is a reliable alternative in networks where OpenVPN or L2TP/IPsec may be blocked or incompatible.

SSL VPNs represent a category of VPNs that use the SSL or TLS protocol to create secure connections between clients and servers. Unlike traditional VPNs that route all traffic through the tunnel, SSL VPNs typically provide access to specific applications or services, making them ideal for remote access to web-based tools, intranet resources, and cloud platforms. SSL VPNs are often implemented using clientless portals accessed through a web browser or through dedicated clients. They offer flexibility and ease of deployment, especially in environments where full tunneling is not required. Because they rely on the same protocols used to secure websites, SSL VPNs can traverse firewalls and proxies with minimal configuration.

VPN technologies and protocols continue to evolve in response to new security challenges, performance demands, and user expectations. While traditional protocols like PPTP and L2TP/IPsec still exist, newer solutions such as WireGuard and OpenVPN are shaping the future of secure remote access. Each protocol comes with its own strengths and trade-offs, influencing its suitability for different scenarios. For organizations, the choice of VPN technology must consider not only security and compatibility but also factors like ease of management, scalability, and support for modern devices and networks. As remote work, global collaboration, and cloud computing become the norm, VPNs will remain critical components of cybersecurity infrastructure, ensuring that data remains protected wherever it travels.

SSL VPN vs IPsec VPN

SSL VPN and IPsec VPN are two prominent technologies used to establish secure, encrypted communication tunnels over public and untrusted networks. Both are designed to protect data in transit, enabling users to access internal systems, applications, and services remotely. However, despite their shared objective of securing network traffic, they operate in fundamentally different ways and are suited to different use cases. The choice between SSL VPN and IPsec VPN depends on multiple factors, including deployment complexity, security requirements, device compatibility, and the nature of the remote access being provided.

IPsec VPN, or Internet Protocol Security Virtual Private Network, is a suite of protocols that operates at the network layer of the OSI model. It provides secure communication by authenticating and encrypting each IP packet in a data stream. IPsec is typically used for site-to-site

VPNs where entire networks need to be securely connected, such as between corporate branch offices or data centers. It can also be configured for remote access by allowing individual users to connect securely to a private network. Because IPsec functions at the IP layer, it can secure virtually all application traffic without requiring changes to the application itself. Once a tunnel is established, all traffic from the client's device can be routed through the encrypted tunnel, providing full access to the internal network.

SSL VPN, or Secure Sockets Layer Virtual Private Network, on the other hand, operates at a higher level in the OSI model, specifically the transport or application layer. It leverages the SSL or TLS protocols, which are the same protocols used to secure web traffic. SSL VPNs can be configured to provide either full-tunnel access, similar to IPsec VPNs, or limited application-specific access. This flexibility is one of the key advantages of SSL VPN technology. Users can access web-based applications, file shares, or email services without needing a full tunnel or a VPN client in many cases. In clientless SSL VPN implementations, access is granted through a web browser, simplifying the user experience and reducing the need for software installation.

One of the primary differences between SSL VPN and IPsec VPN lies in how each handles client access. IPsec VPNs usually require pre-configured VPN client software on the user's device. This software is responsible for initiating the tunnel, handling authentication, and managing encryption. While effective, this approach introduces complexity, especially when supporting a wide range of operating systems and device types. SSL VPNs, in contrast, offer greater accessibility by supporting clientless connections via web browsers. This makes SSL VPNs particularly appealing in environments with a mix of managed and unmanaged devices, such as remote workforces or third-party contractors who may not use company-issued hardware.

Security is another area where the two technologies differ. IPsec VPNs provide strong security through a combination of protocols, including the Internet Key Exchange (IKE) for negotiating session keys and authenticating peers, as well as Encapsulating Security Payload (ESP) for encrypting data. These mechanisms ensure data confidentiality, integrity, and authenticity. IPsec also supports mutual authentication and can be configured to use digital certificates or pre-shared keys. SSL

VPNs also offer strong encryption and authentication, typically relying on TLS to secure the session. However, since SSL VPNs often provide access through a web portal, additional security features such as multi-factor authentication, endpoint compliance checks, and granular access controls are commonly implemented to protect against unauthorized access.

From a performance perspective, both SSL VPN and IPsec VPN can provide reliable and secure communication, but their impact on network performance may differ depending on implementation. IPsec VPNs, due to their operation at the network layer and potential for encrypting all traffic, can introduce latency, especially when routing large volumes of data or supporting many simultaneous connections. SSL VPNs, particularly those providing limited access to specific resources, can reduce overhead and improve performance by encrypting only the necessary application data. Furthermore, SSL VPNs can more easily traverse firewalls and NAT devices since they typically use port 443, which is almost always open for HTTPS traffic. IPsec VPNs, on the other hand, often use protocols and ports that may be blocked by firewalls or require complex NAT traversal techniques such as NAT-T.

Deployment and management considerations also influence the choice between SSL VPN and IPsec VPN. IPsec VPNs may require more extensive configuration on both the client and server sides, including IP routing, firewall rules, and client software distribution. They are well-suited for scenarios where permanent or continuous connectivity between trusted networks is needed. SSL VPNs, with their ease of use and minimal configuration requirements, are better aligned with mobile users, temporary access needs, or environments where centralized control over endpoint devices is limited. Web-based management interfaces and policy-driven access controls make SSL VPNs easier to administer in dynamic, user-centric environments.

Compatibility is another key differentiator. SSL VPNs are generally more adaptable to different operating systems, devices, and network conditions. They are often the preferred choice for supporting remote access from mobile devices, tablets, or kiosks. Because SSL VPNs rely on standard web protocols, they are less likely to encounter issues with restrictive firewalls or corporate proxies. IPsec VPNs, while widely supported on enterprise-grade equipment and operating systems, may face compatibility issues in consumer-grade networks or mobile platforms that lack native IPsec support or require additional configuration.

In summary, SSL VPN and IPsec VPN represent two distinct approaches to secure remote access and inter-network communication. IPsec VPNs are best suited for site-to-site connectivity and full-network access where robust, low-level security and integration with existing network infrastructure are priorities. SSL VPNs excel in providing flexible, user-friendly remote access to specific applications and services, especially in environments with diverse user devices and security policies. Organizations must weigh the trade-offs between complexity, performance, security, and user experience when choosing the most appropriate VPN technology. In many cases, a hybrid approach that employs both SSL VPNs for remote users and IPsec VPNs for network-to-network connections provides the optimal balance between accessibility and control. As security demands evolve and remote work continues to expand, the role of both technologies remains vital in building secure and resilient network architectures.

RADIUS and TACACS+ Authentication Protocols

RADIUS and TACACS+ are two of the most widely used authentication, authorization, and accounting protocols in modern network security architectures. They are employed to control access to network resources by verifying user identities and enforcing security policies. These protocols serve as critical components in centralized authentication systems, especially in environments with large numbers of users, network devices, and access points. Although they share similar purposes, RADIUS and TACACS+ differ significantly in design, functionality, and security features. Understanding their similarities and differences is essential for network administrators who must decide which protocol best meets their organizational needs.

RADIUS, which stands for Remote Authentication Dial-In User Service, was originally developed in the early 1990s by Livingston Enterprises to manage dial-up access to the internet. Since then, it has evolved into a widely adopted protocol used in wireless networks, VPNs, and various enterprise-level remote access systems. RADIUS operates using the User Datagram Protocol, or UDP, typically over port 1812 for authentication and authorization, and port 1813 for accounting. Because it uses UDP, RADIUS is considered lightweight and fast, making it suitable for high-performance applications where speed is a priority.

RADIUS functions by transmitting user credentials and session information from a network access server, such as a wireless controller, VPN gateway, or router, to a centralized RADIUS server. The server authenticates the credentials against a user database, which may be integrated with other systems like Active Directory, LDAP, or local user accounts. If the authentication is successful, the RADIUS server responds with authorization attributes that define the user's level of access. These attributes can include session time limits, VLAN assignments, or specific command sets. In addition to authentication and authorization, RADIUS also provides accounting capabilities, allowing administrators to track session start and stop times, data usage, and other session statistics.

Despite its widespread use, RADIUS has some limitations, particularly in terms of security. One notable issue is that RADIUS encrypts only the user's password in the authentication packet, while other information, such as the username and authorization attributes, is transmitted in plaintext. This creates a potential vulnerability if packets are intercepted on the network. To mitigate this, administrators often deploy RADIUS within secure tunnels or VPNs or rely on IPsec to protect RADIUS traffic. RADIUS also lacks support for complex command authorization and is limited in its ability to control granular user permissions, especially in device management scenarios.

TACACS+, or Terminal Access Controller Access-Control System Plus, was developed by Cisco Systems as an alternative to RADIUS, with enhanced security and more robust support for command-level authorization. TACACS+ operates over TCP, typically using port 49, which provides more reliable communication compared to UDP. One of the defining features of TACACS+ is that it separates the functions of authentication, authorization, and accounting into discrete processes. This modularity gives administrators greater control and flexibility when defining access policies and managing user privileges.

Unlike RADIUS, TACACS+ encrypts the entire payload of the authentication packet, not just the password. This comprehensive encryption significantly enhances security by ensuring that no sensitive data is exposed during transmission. This makes TACACS+ particularly well-suited for use in high-security environments such as government networks, financial institutions, and enterprise data centers. Another key advantage of TACACS+ is its ability to support command-by-command authorization, allowing fine-grained control over which commands a user can execute on a device. This is especially useful in managing network devices like switches and routers, where different levels of administrative privilege are often required.

TACACS+ is commonly integrated into centralized authentication systems alongside user directories and management platforms. It supports a variety of authentication methods, including passwords, challenge-response systems, and multi-factor authentication. Its ability to log detailed user activity, including individual commands issued on network devices, makes it a powerful tool for auditing and compliance. These logging features provide visibility into administrative actions and can be used to detect unauthorized or suspicious behavior in real time.

Despite its strengths, TACACS+ is not as widely supported as RADIUS in some types of equipment, particularly in non-Cisco environments. Many consumer and some enterprise-grade wireless access points, for instance, only support RADIUS. Additionally, because TACACS+ is a proprietary protocol developed by Cisco, its implementations outside of Cisco environments may require third-party solutions or open-source alternatives that mimic its behavior. This can introduce compatibility and support challenges that must be carefully considered during network design and deployment.

In real-world deployments, RADIUS and TACACS+ are often used together, each serving different purposes. For example, RADIUS may be used to authenticate end-user devices connecting to a Wi-Fi network or VPN, while TACACS+ is used to manage administrative access to network infrastructure. This dual-protocol approach allows organizations to leverage the strengths of each system while minimizing their respective limitations. Network policies can be tailored to specific roles, ensuring that end-users have appropriate access to services while network administrators are subject to stricter controls and more detailed auditing.

Modern authentication solutions often integrate RADIUS and TACACS+ with broader identity and access management frameworks. These frameworks may include support for protocols like SAML, OAuth, and OpenID Connect, as well as integration with cloud-based identity providers. By combining traditional network authentication protocols with modern identity services, organizations can implement more dynamic and adaptive security postures. Features such as role-based access control, device posture assessment, and contextual authentication can enhance both security and usability.

The choice between RADIUS and TACACS+ ultimately depends on the specific requirements of the network environment, the types of devices being managed, and the desired level of security. Organizations with a high volume of remote users and a need for efficient, scalable authentication may favor RADIUS for its performance and broad compatibility. On the other hand, organizations that require granular control over administrative actions and enhanced encryption for management traffic may prefer TACACS+ for its robustness and security features. Regardless of the chosen protocol, proper configuration, encryption, and integration with centralized identity systems are essential to ensuring that access control mechanisms remain both effective and secure.

As network architectures continue to evolve with trends such as zero trust, cloud migration, and remote work, the importance of strong and flexible authentication mechanisms becomes even more pronounced. RADIUS and TACACS+ remain foundational technologies in the enforcement of identity and access control, enabling secure interactions across distributed and heterogeneous network environments. Their ongoing relevance reflects the enduring need for reliable, auditable, and policy-driven authentication in the modern digital landscape.

IEEE 802.1X and Network Access Control

IEEE 802.1X is a standard for port-based Network Access Control that plays a central role in securing wired and wireless networks. It provides an authentication mechanism for devices wishing to connect to a LAN or WLAN by using a centralized authentication server, typically via protocols such as RADIUS. As enterprise networks continue to expand and incorporate a wide range of devices, including bring-your-own-device (BYOD) endpoints, printers, and Internet of Things (IoT) components, maintaining visibility and control over what is allowed to access the network has become essential. IEEE 802.1X offers a scalable and flexible approach to ensuring that only authorized and compliant devices can communicate with internal resources.

The operation of IEEE 802.1X involves three primary entities: the supplicant, the authenticator, and the authentication server. The supplicant is the client device seeking to gain access to the network. It can be a laptop, smartphone, tablet, or any other network-enabled device. The authenticator is typically a network switch or wireless access point that controls the physical access to the network. It acts as an intermediary between the supplicant and the authentication server. The authentication server, often running a RADIUS service, validates the credentials provided by the supplicant and informs the authenticator whether access should be granted or denied. This structure creates a robust framework for verifying identity and enforcing security policies at the very point of entry to the network.

When a device connects to a network port that is secured by 802.1X, the port remains in a blocked state until authentication is successful. The authenticator does not allow any traffic other than authentication requests to pass through. The supplicant initiates the authentication by sending an EAPOL (Extensible Authentication Protocol over LAN) message. The authenticator receives this message and forwards it to the authentication server, encapsulated in a RADIUS protocol packet. The server then interacts with a user directory or identity management system, such as Active Directory or LDAP, to verify the user's credentials or the device's identity. If the authentication is successful, the authenticator opens the port, granting access to the network according to predefined policies.

The strength of IEEE 802.1X lies in its support for a wide range of authentication methods through the Extensible Authentication Protocol, or EAP. EAP is a flexible framework that supports multiple authentication mechanisms, including passwords, digital certificates, smart cards, and token-based credentials. EAP-TLS, for example, uses client and server certificates to perform mutual authentication and establish an encrypted session. This method is considered one of the most secure, though it requires a public key infrastructure to issue and manage certificates. EAP-PEAP and EAP-TTLS are also widely used and rely on secure tunnels to protect user credentials during transmission. The ability to support different EAP types makes 802.1X adaptable to various security policies and deployment environments.

Network Access Control, or NAC, extends the capabilities of IEEE 802.1X by adding endpoint posture assessment, policy enforcement, and dynamic network provisioning. While 802.1X focuses on authentication and access control, NAC introduces intelligence that enables the network to evaluate the security posture of a device before granting access. This can include checking whether antivirus software is up to date, whether the operating system has the latest patches, or whether specific applications are installed. Based on the results, NAC can allow full access, redirect the device to a remediation network, or deny access entirely. This dynamic approach enables organizations to enforce security compliance and reduce the risk of compromised or misconfigured devices affecting the network.

The implementation of 802.1X and NAC brings numerous advantages, particularly in large enterprise networks where security and manageability are priorities. One major benefit is the ability to centralize authentication and authorization policies. Instead of configuring access control lists or firewall rules on individual switches and access points, administrators define policies in the authentication server. These policies can then be applied consistently across the network, simplifying management and improving security posture. Additionally, integration with identity directories allows for role-based access control, ensuring that users only receive the network privileges appropriate to their roles or departments.

Another advantage is the support for guest and contractor access management. Many organizations must provide temporary network access to visitors without compromising internal systems. NAC solutions can integrate with captive portals or self-registration systems to securely onboard guest users, assign them to isolated VLANs, and automatically expire their credentials after a set period. This enables flexibility while maintaining control and visibility over network usage. For even tighter security, guest traffic can be limited to specific destinations, such as internet access only, while preventing lateral movement within the internal network.

Despite its advantages, deploying 802.1X and NAC requires careful planning and thorough testing. One of the common challenges is ensuring compatibility with a diverse range of endpoint devices and operating systems. Older devices or embedded systems may not support 802.1X natively or may require manual configuration. To address this, many organizations adopt hybrid approaches that combine 802.1X with MAC authentication bypass or web-based authentication methods. Additionally, organizations must ensure that their authentication infrastructure is highly available and scalable. If the authentication server becomes unavailable or overloaded, it can cause legitimate users to be denied access, leading to disruptions in productivity.

Proper certificate management is also critical in environments that use EAP-TLS. Certificates must be issued, renewed, and revoked in a timely manner to ensure secure communication and prevent unauthorized access. Automated certificate enrollment and lifecycle management tools can simplify this process, reducing administrative burden and minimizing the risk of expired or compromised certificates. User training and communication are equally important, especially in environments transitioning from open access to 802.1X-controlled networks. Users must understand how to authenticate and what to expect during the onboarding process to avoid confusion and support tickets.

Monitoring and logging are essential components of any 802.1X and NAC deployment. The authentication server and network devices should log all access attempts, including successes, failures, and any changes in access policies. These logs provide valuable insights into network activity, help detect unauthorized access attempts, and support forensic investigations in the event of a security incident. Many NAC solutions also include dashboards and reporting tools that offer real-time visibility into network health, device compliance, and user behavior.

As cybersecurity threats continue to evolve, controlling who and what is allowed onto the network becomes more critical than ever. IEEE 802.1X and Network Access Control provide the tools necessary to implement granular, identity-based access policies and enforce them at the network edge. By combining strong authentication, endpoint compliance checking, and centralized policy enforcement, these technologies create a dynamic and responsive security architecture that can adapt to new challenges while maintaining the performance and availability of the network. Their role in securing enterprise environments, enabling BYOD policies, and supporting compliance requirements makes them foundational components of modern network defense strategies.

WPA2 and WPA3 Wireless Security

WPA2 and WPA3 represent two generations of wireless security protocols developed to protect Wi-Fi networks from unauthorized access and ensure the confidentiality and integrity of data transmitted over the air. Wireless networks are inherently more vulnerable than their wired counterparts because radio signals can be intercepted without physical access to network infrastructure. To mitigate this risk, strong encryption and authentication mechanisms are essential. WPA2, or Wi-Fi Protected Access 2, became the standard for wireless security in the mid-2000s and remained dominant for over a decade. It addressed many of the shortcomings of its predecessor, WPA, and provided robust security for both personal and enterprise environments. However, as new attack techniques emerged and the demand for even stronger security grew, WPA3 was introduced to offer improved protections and modern cryptographic features designed for the evolving landscape of wireless communication.

WPA2 introduced the use of the Advanced Encryption Standard, or AES, with the Counter Mode with Cipher Block Chaining Message Authentication Code Protocol, commonly known as CCMP. This replaced the older and flawed Temporal Key Integrity Protocol, or TKIP, which was susceptible to various attacks. AES-CCMP provided significantly stronger data encryption and integrity protection, making it the cornerstone of WPA2's security model. WPA2 operates in two primary modes: WPA2-Personal and WPA2-Enterprise. In WPA2-Personal, a pre-shared key, or PSK, is used for authentication. This key is manually configured on all devices and used to derive encryption keys. While convenient for home or small office networks, WPA2-PSK relies heavily on the strength and secrecy of the shared password. If the password is weak or disclosed, the security of the network is compromised.

WPA2-Enterprise, on the other hand, uses 802.1X authentication in combination with a RADIUS server to authenticate users individually. Each user is granted a unique encryption key after successful authentication, enhancing both security and manageability. This mode is preferred in business and institutional environments, where user accountability and policy enforcement are important. WPA2-Enterprise supports a variety of EAP methods, including EAP-TLS, EAP-TTLS, and PEAP, allowing for the use of certificates, tokens, or username and password combinations. This flexibility, along with centralized user management and logging, makes WPA2-Enterprise a comprehensive solution for securing wireless networks in professional settings.

Despite the robustness of WPA2, several vulnerabilities have been discovered over time. One of the most significant was the Key Reinstallation Attack, or KRACK, revealed in 2017. This attack exploited a flaw in the four-way handshake process used to establish encryption keys between a client and an access point. By manipulating handshake messages, an attacker could force the client to reinstall an already-in-use key, resetting packet counters and allowing for decryption of data packets. Although patches were released for most affected systems, KRACK highlighted the limitations of WPA2 and the need for a more resilient protocol.

WPA3 was developed by the Wi-Fi Alliance to address these limitations and to offer stronger protection in both personal and enterprise networks. One of the core improvements in WPA3-Personal is the introduction of Simultaneous Authentication of Equals, or SAE, which replaces the pre-shared key method used in WPA2. SAE is a password-authenticated key exchange that resists offline dictionary attacks and provides forward secrecy. Unlike WPA2-PSK, where a captured handshake could be brute-forced offline, SAE ensures that each authentication attempt must occur in real time, limiting the effectiveness of password-guessing attacks. This greatly enhances the security of home networks, especially those with relatively weak passwords.

WPA3-Enterprise builds on the strong foundation of WPA2-Enterprise by requiring support for 192-bit cryptographic strength in high-security networks. This includes the use of AES-GCM for encryption, SHA-384 for integrity, and elliptic curve cryptography for key exchange. These enhancements are particularly relevant for government, financial, and healthcare sectors, where the confidentiality of sensitive data is paramount. Additionally, WPA3 improves the robustness of the handshake protocol, eliminating vulnerabilities like KRACK and making the key exchange process more resilient to manipulation and replay attacks.

Another significant addition introduced with WPA3 is Protected Management Frames, or PMF. While optional in WPA2, PMF is mandatory in WPA3, providing encryption and integrity for management frames such as disassociation and deauthentication messages. This prevents attackers from spoofing these frames to forcibly disconnect clients from the network, a common tactic used in denial-of-service attacks. By securing both data and control traffic, WPA3 provides a more comprehensive security model for modern Wi-Fi environments.

WPA3 also introduces a transitional mode to aid in deployment. In this mode, access points can support both WPA2 and WPA3 clients simultaneously, allowing organizations to gradually migrate their infrastructure while maintaining backward compatibility. This is important because the adoption of WPA3 requires support on both the client and the access point. Many older devices cannot be upgraded to

WPA3 due to hardware limitations, making a staged deployment strategy necessary for most environments.

In addition to improvements in core protocols, WPA3 includes support for Enhanced Open networks through Opportunistic Wireless Encryption, or OWE. Traditional open Wi-Fi networks, such as those found in cafes, airports, and hotels, do not encrypt data, exposing users to eavesdropping and man-in-the-middle attacks. OWE provides encryption for open networks without requiring user authentication or a password. Each client establishes a unique encryption key with the access point during connection, ensuring that traffic between them is private even though the network remains open to the public. This feature is a major step forward in improving baseline security for users who connect to public Wi-Fi.

As with any security technology, the effectiveness of WPA2 and WPA3 depends on proper implementation and configuration. Network administrators must ensure that strong passwords or certificates are used, that firmware is regularly updated, and that features such as PMF and SAE are correctly enabled. Users should also be educated about the risks of connecting to untrusted networks and encouraged to verify the authenticity of access points. In enterprise environments, integrating wireless authentication with identity management systems and endpoint compliance tools can further strengthen access control and visibility.

The evolution from WPA2 to WPA3 reflects the growing complexity of wireless networking and the increasing sophistication of threats. As more devices connect wirelessly—from smartphones and laptops to smart home systems and industrial sensors—the need for reliable and future-proof security becomes more pressing. WPA3 delivers critical enhancements that address known weaknesses, align with modern cryptographic standards, and provide a stronger foundation for secure wireless communication. Its adoption marks an important milestone in the ongoing effort to protect digital data as it moves across the invisible paths of the airwaves, securing not only individual users but the broader ecosystems they depend on.

Firewalls and Protocol Filtering

Firewalls and protocol filtering play a critical role in modern network security, acting as the first line of defense against unauthorized access and cyber threats. As networks have evolved to support more complex applications and services, the need for sophisticated filtering mechanisms has grown accordingly. Firewalls serve not only as barriers between trusted internal networks and untrusted external environments, such as the internet, but also as active managers of network traffic, inspecting and deciding which packets are allowed or denied based on a set of predefined rules. These rules are designed to enforce the organization's security policies, ensuring that only authorized traffic can pass through the network perimeter.

At the core of a firewall's functionality is its ability to inspect data packets, which are the basic units of communication over a network. A data packet typically contains header information and a payload. The header includes details such as the source and destination IP addresses, the protocol being used, and the port numbers involved in the communication. Firewalls analyze this header information to determine whether a packet should be allowed to enter or leave the network. Traditional firewalls operated primarily at the network and transport layers of the OSI model, filtering traffic based on IP addresses, ports, and protocols. These were known as packet-filtering firewalls. While effective to a degree, they lacked the capability to inspect the contents of the packet payloads or to understand the context of communications.

To address these limitations, more advanced firewall technologies were developed. Stateful inspection firewalls represented a significant evolution by tracking the state of active connections and making decisions based on the context of the traffic. For example, if a user initiates a connection to a web server, the firewall allows return traffic from the server only if it matches the state of the original request. This significantly reduces the risk of certain types of attacks, such as unsolicited inbound traffic attempting to exploit vulnerabilities. Further advancements led to the development of application-layer firewalls, also known as next-generation firewalls (NGFWs), which inspect traffic at a deeper level and can recognize and enforce policies based on specific applications, users, and even content types.

Protocol filtering extends the capabilities of firewalls by allowing or denying traffic based on the specific protocols being used. Protocols are standardized sets of rules that govern how data is transmitted and received over a network. Examples include HTTP for web traffic, SMTP for email, and FTP for file transfers. While these protocols are essential for communication, they can also be exploited by attackers to penetrate systems, exfiltrate data, or deliver malicious payloads. By implementing protocol filtering, network administrators can tightly control which types of traffic are permitted, reducing the attack surface and preventing the misuse of legitimate protocols for malicious purposes.

One key advantage of protocol filtering is its granularity. Instead of merely blocking or allowing entire ports, administrators can define rules that inspect protocol behavior more precisely. For instance, while HTTP traffic might be generally permitted, specific HTTP methods such as PUT or DELETE can be blocked to prevent users from performing actions that could compromise the integrity of web applications. Similarly, protocol filtering can be used to block certain commands within FTP sessions or to restrict email attachments to particular file types. This level of control enables organizations to tailor their security posture to the specific needs of their environment, ensuring that only the necessary communication is allowed and everything else is denied or scrutinized.

Modern firewalls also incorporate deep packet inspection (DPI) techniques to analyze the payload of packets in addition to header information. This allows for even more precise protocol filtering, as the firewall can understand the full context of the data being transmitted. DPI can detect anomalies, policy violations, and potential threats embedded within application-layer data, such as malware hidden in HTTP responses or unauthorized data transfers in encrypted sessions. Coupled with intrusion detection and prevention systems (IDPS), these capabilities form a powerful defense mechanism that not only filters unwanted traffic but also actively detects and responds to threats in real-time.

The implementation of firewalls and protocol filtering is not limited to the network perimeter. With the rise of cloud computing, mobile devices, and remote work, organizations have had to extend these protections beyond traditional boundaries. This has given rise to distributed firewalls and microsegmentation strategies, where filtering policies are enforced within the internal network or even at the level of individual workloads. Cloud-native firewalls integrate with virtualized environments and offer scalable, policy-driven controls that adapt to dynamic infrastructure. In this context, protocol filtering remains essential, ensuring that traffic between virtual machines or containers adheres to security policies and cannot be exploited by attackers who may have breached part of the system.

Another important aspect of protocol filtering is its role in compliance and auditing. Many industries are subject to regulations that require strict control over data flows, including who can access specific services and how sensitive information is transmitted. Firewalls equipped with protocol filtering capabilities can help organizations meet these requirements by enforcing access controls and generating detailed logs of network activity. These logs provide visibility into who is using what protocols, from where, and for what purpose, enabling security teams to monitor for suspicious activity and demonstrate compliance during audits.

Despite their many benefits, firewalls and protocol filtering must be properly configured and maintained to be effective. Misconfigurations, such as overly permissive rules or outdated filtering policies, can create security gaps that attackers may exploit. Regular reviews, updates, and testing of firewall rules are essential to maintaining a strong security posture. Additionally, as encrypted traffic becomes more prevalent, firewalls must adapt to inspect and filter protocols such as HTTPS without compromising performance or privacy. This may involve decrypting and re-encrypting traffic, a process that requires careful handling of encryption keys and adherence to privacy regulations.

In summary, firewalls and protocol filtering are indispensable components of any comprehensive cybersecurity strategy. They provide robust mechanisms for controlling network traffic, enforcing security policies, and mitigating threats before they can reach critical systems. As the threat landscape continues to evolve, so too must the capabilities and deployment models of firewalls, ensuring that they remain effective in protecting modern, distributed, and dynamic IT environments.

Deep Packet Inspection and SSL Inspection

Deep Packet Inspection (DPI) and SSL Inspection are two critical technologies in the modern cybersecurity landscape, enabling organizations to analyze network traffic with a high degree of precision and visibility. These inspection techniques go far beyond the capabilities of traditional firewalls and network security devices, which typically rely on header information such as IP addresses, ports, and basic protocol types to determine whether to allow or block traffic. By contrast, DPI and SSL Inspection operate at much deeper levels of the OSI model, allowing for the examination of the contents of data packets and encrypted communications, respectively. As cyber threats continue to grow in sophistication, these technologies have become essential tools for detecting and preventing a wide range of malicious activities that would otherwise evade conventional security measures.

Deep Packet Inspection refers to the process of examining the entire contents of network packets, including both the header and the payload. This level of scrutiny allows security systems to not only identify the applications or services being used but also to detect patterns and anomalies within the data itself. DPI is especially valuable in identifying threats that are hidden within legitimate traffic. For instance, a file attachment that appears to be a harmless document might actually contain embedded malware. Traditional filtering methods might allow such a file to pass through unchecked, but DPI can analyze the file's structure and identify indicators of compromise based on known malware signatures or behavioral analysis.

Furthermore, DPI plays a significant role in enforcing organizational policies related to acceptable use, data loss prevention, and application control. Organizations can use DPI to block access to certain types of content, such as streaming media or social media platforms, during work hours. It can also be used to monitor for attempts to transfer sensitive data outside the organization, whether through email, file-sharing services, or even encrypted tunnels. DPI can identify keywords, data formats, or file types that indicate the presence of confidential or regulated information, triggering alerts or automatic blocks to prevent unauthorized disclosure. This makes DPI not only a security tool but also a compliance and productivity management asset.

One of the main challenges DPI faces is its impact on performance. Inspecting every packet in detail requires significant processing power, especially in high-throughput environments such as data centers or large enterprise networks. Advances in hardware acceleration and parallel processing have helped mitigate this issue, but organizations must still carefully balance the depth of inspection with the performance demands of their network. Additionally, DPI can raise privacy concerns, particularly when used to inspect personal communications or in jurisdictions with strong data protection regulations. As such, it must be deployed with clear policies, transparency, and, where applicable, user consent.

While DPI provides deep visibility into unencrypted traffic, the rise of encryption has created new challenges. Today, a significant portion of internet traffic is encrypted using protocols like SSL and its successor, TLS. This encryption protects data from eavesdropping and tampering, but it also renders traditional inspection tools blind to the contents of the communication. Attackers have increasingly taken advantage of this blind spot, hiding malware, command-and-control traffic, and data exfiltration attempts within encrypted channels. To address this issue, SSL Inspection, also known as HTTPS Inspection, was developed.

SSL Inspection involves decrypting and analyzing encrypted traffic as it passes through a security appliance, then re-encrypting it before sending it to its final destination. This allows the security system to inspect the contents of encrypted sessions just as it would unencrypted traffic. With SSL Inspection, organizations can apply their full range of security controls—including DPI, antivirus scanning, and data loss prevention—to encrypted traffic, closing a major gap in their defenses. This is especially important in scenarios where employees access web-based applications, cloud services, or external websites that may be compromised or serve as vectors for advanced persistent threats.

The implementation of SSL Inspection is technically complex and requires careful planning. First, the security appliance performing the inspection must be able to impersonate the original server by generating and presenting a substitute SSL certificate to the client. To avoid security warnings, organizations must configure all client devices to trust the certificate authority used by the inspection device. Once the traffic is decrypted, the device performs its analysis and applies any necessary security policies before re-encrypting the traffic and forwarding it to the original destination server. This process is seamless to the user but must be managed carefully to maintain performance and trust.

Despite its advantages, SSL Inspection raises important ethical and legal considerations. Since it involves intercepting and decrypting private communications, it can potentially violate user privacy or regulatory requirements. Organizations must ensure that SSL Inspection is deployed in a way that respects privacy laws and internal policies. This may involve excluding certain types of traffic from inspection, such as banking or healthcare communications, or applying inspection only to managed devices where users have given consent. Transparency is key, and organizations should communicate clearly with users about the scope and purpose of SSL Inspection.

Performance is another challenge. Decrypting and re-encrypting traffic is resource-intensive and can introduce latency if not properly optimized. To address this, modern SSL Inspection solutions often incorporate hardware acceleration, intelligent traffic segmentation, and policy-based bypass rules that skip inspection for trusted or low-risk destinations. These optimizations help maintain a balance between security and user experience, ensuring that critical inspection capabilities do not come at the cost of network efficiency.

Both Deep Packet Inspection and SSL Inspection are constantly evolving in response to changes in technology and threat landscapes. As attackers develop more sophisticated methods of evading detection—such as encrypted malware, steganography, and polymorphic payloads—security solutions must become more intelligent and adaptive. Machine learning and behavior-based analysis are increasingly integrated into DPI engines to detect anomalies that do not match known signatures. Similarly, SSL Inspection systems are being designed to recognize malicious behavior patterns even when payloads are obfuscated or disguised within legitimate-looking traffic.

Together, DPI and SSL Inspection form a powerful combination for securing modern networks. By providing visibility into both encrypted and unencrypted communications, they enable organizations to detect threats, enforce policies, and safeguard sensitive data across increasingly complex digital environments. Their proper implementation, however, requires a strategic approach that balances security, performance, and privacy. As organizations continue to embrace cloud services, remote work, and mobile access, the need for deep and intelligent traffic inspection will only grow, making DPI and SSL Inspection indispensable components of future-ready cybersecurity architectures.

Security in Software-Defined Networking (SDN)

Security in Software-Defined Networking (SDN) is an essential topic in the evolving landscape of network architecture. As organizations seek greater flexibility, scalability, and automation, SDN has emerged as a transformative approach to managing and configuring networks. By decoupling the control plane from the data plane, SDN allows centralized control over network behavior through programmable interfaces. This architectural shift offers numerous benefits, including more dynamic traffic management and the ability to respond to changing business needs with unprecedented speed. However, it also introduces new security challenges and vulnerabilities that must be addressed with careful design and proactive defense mechanisms.

One of the key characteristics of SDN is its centralized controller, which serves as the brain of the network. This controller has a global view of the entire network and makes decisions about how traffic should flow, instructing individual network devices on how to forward packets. While this centralization enables greater efficiency and agility, it also creates a potential single point of failure. If the SDN controller is compromised, misconfigured, or overwhelmed by malicious traffic, the entire network can be disrupted or manipulated. Attackers could exploit vulnerabilities in the controller's software or communication channels to intercept, alter, or drop data flows, posing serious risks to confidentiality, integrity, and availability.

To mitigate these risks, securing the SDN controller is a top priority. Access to the controller must be strictly controlled using strong authentication and authorization mechanisms. Role-based access controls can help ensure that only authorized administrators can perform specific functions, reducing the risk of insider threats or accidental misconfigurations. Encryption should be used to protect communication between the controller and network devices, preventing eavesdropping or tampering by unauthorized entities. Additionally, the controller should be hardened against exploitation through rigorous software testing, vulnerability scanning, and regular updates to patch security flaws.

Another area of concern in SDN environments is the communication between the control plane and the data plane. This interaction typically occurs using standardized protocols such as OpenFlow, which allows the controller to install, modify, or delete flow rules on switches. If attackers gain access to the network and inject malicious flow rules or manipulate legitimate traffic, they can bypass security controls, reroute data, or cause denial of service. Protecting these communication channels with encryption and message integrity checks is essential. Moreover, monitoring and auditing flow rule changes can help detect unusual or unauthorized behavior that may indicate an ongoing attack.

The programmability of SDN also introduces security concerns related to application development and deployment. SDN controllers often expose northbound APIs that allow developers to create custom applications that influence network behavior. These applications can automate tasks such as load balancing, intrusion detection, or bandwidth allocation. However, if these applications are poorly written, lack proper input validation, or are vulnerable to injection attacks, they can become vectors for exploiting the SDN environment. It is crucial to adopt secure coding practices, perform thorough code reviews, and validate applications before they are deployed to production systems.

Despite these challenges, SDN also offers unique opportunities to enhance security through its centralized intelligence and dynamic control. For instance, network administrators can use SDN to implement real-time threat detection and response. By analyzing traffic patterns across the entire network, the controller can quickly identify anomalies that may indicate a security incident, such as a sudden spike in traffic, lateral movement between devices, or attempts to access restricted services. Once a threat is identified, the controller can automatically isolate compromised hosts, reroute traffic to quarantine zones, or apply rate-limiting to mitigate the impact of attacks. This level of responsiveness is difficult to achieve in traditional networks where control is distributed and reactive measures take more time.

In addition, SDN facilitates the implementation of network segmentation and microsegmentation, which are powerful strategies for limiting the spread of threats. In a traditional network, segmentation often requires manual configuration of VLANs, firewalls, and access control lists, which can be complex and error-prone. With SDN, segmentation policies can be defined programmatically and enforced consistently across the network. Administrators can create logical segments for different departments, applications, or user groups, and dynamically adjust access policies as needed. This granular control reduces the attack surface and limits the ability of attackers to move laterally once they gain access.

Another benefit of SDN is the ability to integrate with other security tools and orchestrate coordinated defenses. For example, SDN controllers can interface with intrusion prevention systems, firewalls, and security information and event management platforms to share threat intelligence and automate responses. When a threat is detected by one system, the controller can be notified and take immediate action to block malicious traffic or update flow rules. This level of integration enhances situational awareness and reduces the time between detection and mitigation, which is crucial in minimizing damage during an attack.

The adoption of SDN in cloud environments and data centers also underscores the need for robust security strategies. Cloud service providers often rely on SDN to manage virtual networks and tenant isolation. In these multi-tenant environments, a breach in SDN security could result in unauthorized access to other customers' data or services. Ensuring the integrity of the SDN control plane and enforcing strict policy controls is essential to maintaining trust and meeting compliance requirements. Additionally, visibility into virtual traffic flows must be maintained to detect policy violations and respond to incidents in real time.

While SDN represents a significant shift in how networks are built and managed, it does not eliminate the need for traditional security best practices. Rather, it complements them by enabling more adaptive and automated defenses. Firewalls, intrusion detection systems, and endpoint protection remain vital components of a comprehensive security architecture, and their effectiveness can be enhanced through integration with the SDN controller. Security policies must be designed with an understanding of how SDN operates, and all stakeholders—from network engineers to application developers—must be trained to recognize the unique challenges and opportunities it presents.

As SDN continues to mature, industry standards and best practices are emerging to guide secure implementations. Organizations considering or currently deploying SDN must prioritize security from the outset, incorporating it into the design, deployment, and ongoing management of the network. The dynamic and programmable nature of SDN can be harnessed to build more resilient and responsive networks, but this potential can only be realized if security is treated as a fundamental element of the architecture. By understanding the specific threats associated with SDN and applying layered, proactive defenses, organizations can embrace this technology while safeguarding their critical assets and ensuring the trustworthiness of their network infrastructure.

Protocols in Zero Trust Architectures

Protocols in Zero Trust Architectures play a foundational role in enabling secure, identity-centric access to systems, data, and services across modern digital environments. Zero Trust is not a single product or tool but rather a comprehensive security model that operates on the principle of never assuming trust, regardless of whether access requests originate inside or outside the organizational perimeter. In this model, verification is continuous and based on a combination of identity, context, and policy enforcement. To implement this approach effectively, specific protocols are required to manage authentication, authorization, encryption, and communication across distributed systems. These protocols ensure that every interaction is validated, logged, and restricted according to the principle of least privilege.

At the heart of Zero Trust is strong identity verification, which is facilitated by protocols like OAuth 2.0 and OpenID Connect. OAuth 2.0 is a widely adopted authorization framework that allows users to grant limited access to their resources without sharing credentials. It enables token-based access, which is crucial in a Zero Trust setting, where fine-grained control over what resources can be accessed and for how long is essential. OpenID Connect builds on top of OAuth 2.0 to add authentication, allowing systems to confirm a user's identity using identity tokens. Together, these protocols enable single sign-on experiences while maintaining strict access boundaries and ensuring that identity assertions are verifiable and time-limited.

In addition to these identity protocols, Zero Trust relies heavily on Transport Layer Security, or TLS, to ensure encrypted communication between all endpoints. TLS is essential for preserving the confidentiality and integrity of data as it moves across potentially hostile networks. Unlike traditional models that assumed security within the corporate perimeter, Zero Trust requires encryption for all traffic, even within internal networks. This means that every connection between services, devices, or users must be protected with TLS to prevent data leakage, tampering, or interception. Certificates play a key role in TLS, and in a Zero Trust architecture, certificate lifecycle management must be automated and tightly integrated with policy enforcement systems to reduce the risk of expired or misconfigured certificates.

Mutual TLS, or mTLS, takes encryption a step further by requiring both client and server to authenticate each other using certificates. This is a critical element of Zero Trust, as it prevents unauthorized devices or services from establishing communication even if they are within the network. mTLS enforces a mutual identity check, which aligns with the core Zero Trust concept of continuous verification. This protocol is especially useful in microservices architectures, where hundreds or thousands of services may interact in complex ways, and each interaction must be verified for authenticity and authorization. Implementing mTLS across an environment requires proper certificate authority infrastructure, service identity management, and a clear strategy for certificate rotation and revocation.

Another protocol that plays a vital role in Zero Trust is Security Assertion Markup Language, or SAML. Although it is an older standard compared to OpenID Connect, SAML is still widely used, especially in enterprise environments for enabling single sign-on and federated identity management. It allows users to authenticate with one identity provider and then access multiple services without reauthenticating. In a Zero Trust framework, SAML can serve as a bridge for legacy systems that need to integrate with newer identity and access control policies. By ensuring that SAML assertions are signed and validated properly, organizations can maintain secure access across both modern and legacy platforms.

Zero Trust also requires detailed access control decisions based on contextual information such as device health, location, and behavior. To support this, protocols like RADIUS and TACACS+ are used to enforce network access control, particularly for infrastructure and administrative access. These protocols allow for centralized authentication, authorization, and accounting, enabling organizations to enforce granular access policies based on role, device posture, or network segment. While RADIUS is more commonly used for user access control, TACACS+ is often favored for administrative tasks due to its separation of authentication and authorization functions. Both play an important role in enforcing Zero Trust principles at the network access layer.

Device health verification is another critical element of Zero Trust, and protocols such as Network Access Control (NAC) and 802.1X are often employed to ensure that only compliant and secure devices are permitted to access network resources. These protocols integrate with endpoint detection and response systems to assess device status in real time, such as whether antivirus software is running, if the operating system is up to date, or if the device is enrolled in a mobile device management system. Based on these factors, access can be granted or denied, and remediation steps can be enforced automatically to bring devices into compliance before access is allowed.

The implementation of Zero Trust also benefits from the use of policy decision and policy enforcement protocols. For example, the Extensible Access Control Markup Language (XACML) allows organizations to define rich access control policies and evaluate them dynamically. With XACML, access decisions are made based on a combination of user attributes, resource attributes, and environmental conditions. This is well suited to Zero Trust, which relies on real-time context and adaptive responses rather than static access lists. The enforcement of these decisions is handled by Policy Enforcement Points (PEPs) embedded within applications or gateways that intercept access requests and consult a centralized Policy Decision Point (PDP) before granting access.

Service Mesh technologies, such as Istio and Linkerd, use these protocols and add orchestration capabilities to apply Zero Trust principles across microservices environments. They embed mTLS, policy enforcement, and telemetry at the infrastructure layer, allowing fine-grained control and visibility over east-west traffic. Within a service mesh, every service call is authenticated, authorized, and encrypted, reducing the risk of unauthorized access or lateral movement by threat actors. These capabilities are crucial for Zero Trust architectures operating in cloud-native environments where traditional perimeter-based defenses are ineffective.

Zero Trust is not limited to enterprise systems but extends to user devices, cloud platforms, and third-party integrations. Protocols such as SCIM (System for Cross-domain Identity Management) help manage identity lifecycle across multiple platforms, ensuring that user access is promptly updated when roles change or employment ends. Similarly, protocols supporting logging and auditing, like syslog and Security Information and Event Management (SIEM) standards, are essential for maintaining observability and accountability. By collecting detailed logs of every access request, policy decision, and enforcement action, organizations gain the insights needed to detect anomalies, investigate incidents, and demonstrate compliance with regulatory requirements.

By orchestrating these diverse protocols into a cohesive security architecture, Zero Trust enables continuous, adaptive, and context-aware access control. Each protocol contributes a piece of the puzzle, from authenticating users and devices, to encrypting data in motion, to enforcing dynamic policies and recording all activity for forensic analysis. The careful integration and management of these protocols form the backbone of a resilient, secure, and future-ready Zero Trust environment that can withstand the complexities of modern digital operations.

TLS in Microservices and Containers

TLS in microservices and containers is a cornerstone of secure communication in cloud-native architectures. As organizations increasingly adopt containerization and microservices to improve scalability, agility, and deployment speed, the attack surface also expands, making security a top concern. In such distributed environments, services often communicate with each other over the network, exchanging sensitive information such as authentication tokens, user data, and configuration secrets. Transport Layer Security, or TLS, provides the encryption and integrity assurance needed to secure these communications, ensuring that data remains confidential and untampered throughout its journey between services.

In traditional monolithic applications, most internal communication occurs in-process, meaning security was often enforced primarily at the perimeter. However, in microservices architectures, a single application is broken into many smaller, independent services that each perform a specific business function. These services interact through APIs, usually over HTTP or gRPC, and each interaction represents a potential point of exposure. Containers, as the underlying runtime environment for microservices, make it easy to deploy and scale these components across clusters, but they also increase the number of endpoints and connections that must be secured. TLS ensures that all data exchanged over these connections is encrypted, preventing unauthorized parties from intercepting or modifying it, even within the internal network.

The application of TLS in microservices and container environments introduces both technical challenges and operational complexities. One of the primary requirements is that each service participating in secure communication must possess a valid digital certificate. This certificate identifies the service and establishes trust between the client and the server during the TLS handshake. In environments with hundreds or thousands of ephemeral containers and services spinning up and down constantly, manually managing these certificates is impractical. Therefore, certificate management must be automated. Solutions like service meshes help automate certificate issuance, renewal, and revocation using built-in Certificate Authorities (CAs) or integration with external PKI systems.

Service meshes such as Istio, Linkerd, and Consul have become critical enablers of TLS in containerized microservices. These platforms abstract the complexity of managing TLS connections by inserting sidecar proxies alongside each service. These proxies intercept inbound and outbound traffic, automatically encrypting it with TLS and authenticating peers using mutual TLS, or mTLS. With mTLS, both the client and server present certificates during the handshake, providing mutual authentication and ensuring that only authorized services can communicate with one another. This is especially important in microservices environments, where services are often dynamically scheduled and IP-based access controls are unreliable.

The use of mTLS in microservices enhances security by eliminating blind trust between services. It prevents unauthorized access, reduces the risk of man-in-the-middle attacks, and ensures that compromised or rogue services cannot impersonate legitimate ones. Each service identity is tied to its certificate, which can be scoped to include attributes such as the namespace, deployment, or specific service name. These identities are then used to define fine-grained access policies that determine which services are allowed to talk to which others. For example, a payment service might only be allowed to communicate with the order service and not with the user profile service. These policies can be centrally managed and dynamically updated without modifying the individual services.

Another critical aspect of TLS in containers and microservices is key management. TLS relies on cryptographic keys to establish secure connections, and the protection of these keys is vital. Keys must be stored securely, rotated frequently, and never hard-coded into application containers or configuration files. Secret management solutions like HashiCorp Vault, Kubernetes Secrets, and cloud-native secret stores help manage these sensitive materials. Integration with service meshes or orchestration platforms ensures that keys and certificates are securely delivered to services when needed and removed when no longer necessary.

Latency and performance are often raised as concerns when implementing TLS at scale. Encrypting and decrypting data, performing certificate validation, and managing sessions all introduce computational overhead. However, these costs are typically outweighed by the security benefits, and modern CPUs with hardware acceleration for cryptographic operations significantly reduce the performance impact. Moreover, service meshes and load balancers often include TLS termination and optimization features that help mitigate these concerns. Session resumption, connection pooling, and other techniques allow services to maintain efficient, encrypted connections without repeatedly incurring the cost of full TLS handshakes.

TLS also plays a role in securing ingress and egress traffic in containerized environments. When external clients access services hosted in a Kubernetes cluster, ingress controllers act as the entry point and must terminate TLS connections securely. Certificates used at the ingress must be managed carefully to avoid expired or misconfigured certificates that could cause outages or security warnings. Automated tools like cert-manager for Kubernetes can provision and renew certificates from trusted authorities such as Let's Encrypt. Similarly, when services make calls to external APIs or services outside the cluster, egress gateways must enforce TLS to ensure secure outbound communication. These gateways can also inspect and log traffic, apply rate-limiting, and implement data loss prevention policies.

Logging and monitoring TLS connections is essential for observability and incident response. Metrics related to handshake success rates, cipher suite usage, and certificate validity provide insight into the health and security of the communication infrastructure. Centralized logging solutions can collect data from service proxies, load balancers, and ingress controllers, offering a comprehensive view of encrypted traffic flows. In the event of a security incident, this data is invaluable for tracing the path of compromised traffic, identifying misconfigurations, and understanding the scope of the breach. Continuous monitoring also helps ensure compliance with regulatory frameworks that require encryption of data in transit.

TLS is not a silver bullet, and its implementation must be complemented by secure software development practices, proper network segmentation, and runtime protection for containers. Vulnerabilities within services themselves, such as insecure APIs or exploitable code, can still be abused even if the communication is encrypted. Nonetheless, TLS provides a strong foundation for securing communication between microservices, and its correct implementation significantly reduces the risk of data exposure and unauthorized access.

As container orchestration and microservices become standard in enterprise IT, the role of TLS will continue to grow in importance. The ability to automatically encrypt service-to-service communication, verify service identities, and enforce access control policies enables organizations to build secure and resilient distributed systems. By integrating TLS deeply into the infrastructure through automation and orchestration tools, organizations can maintain a consistent and reliable security posture, even as their environments become more dynamic, complex, and interconnected.

Protocol Security in IoT Environments

Protocol security in IoT environments is one of the most critical aspects of safeguarding modern interconnected systems. The Internet of Things has introduced an ecosystem where billions of devices interact continuously across various sectors, from industrial automation and smart homes to healthcare systems and critical infrastructure. These devices often have limited processing power, constrained memory, and specialized operating systems, making traditional security approaches difficult to implement. In this context, securing the communication protocols that facilitate data exchange between IoT devices, gateways, and cloud services becomes vital. Without robust protocol-level security, attackers can intercept, manipulate, or spoof messages, leading to data breaches, unauthorized control, or denial of service attacks.

IoT environments rely on a diverse set of communication protocols, each with its unique characteristics, strengths, and vulnerabilities. Many of these protocols were originally designed with performance and low-power consumption in mind, rather than security. For instance, protocols like MQTT, CoAP, and Zigbee are optimized for small payloads, low overhead, and real-time communication. However, without additional security layers, they become susceptible to a range of threats. MQTT, a lightweight messaging protocol often used in industrial and home automation, lacks built-in encryption and authentication. To secure MQTT communications, TLS must be implemented as an external layer, encrypting data in transit and authenticating both brokers and clients. Yet, due to resource constraints, many IoT devices are incapable of handling full TLS stacks, leaving them exposed unless alternative lightweight security mechanisms are applied.

CoAP, or the Constrained Application Protocol, was developed specifically for constrained devices and networks. While it mimics the functionality of HTTP and is used widely in IoT, especially in constrained RESTful environments, it also suffers from similar issues. CoAP is typically deployed over UDP, which itself lacks any native security features. To secure CoAP traffic, DTLS, or Datagram Transport Layer Security, is commonly used. DTLS provides similar protections as TLS but is designed for the datagram-oriented nature of UDP. However, implementing DTLS correctly is complex and prone to misconfigurations. Many devices that claim DTLS support either fail to validate certificates properly or allow weak cipher suites, undermining the purpose of encryption.

Zigbee and Z-Wave, two popular protocols for short-range, low-power communications in smart home devices, introduce yet another set of challenges. These protocols often operate on mesh networks, where devices relay messages between each other. While Zigbee has built-in security mechanisms such as AES-128 encryption, key management is often poorly implemented. Default keys, hardcoded credentials, and lack of secure key exchange mechanisms expose the network to key leakage and spoofing attacks. Attackers who gain access to one node can potentially infiltrate the entire mesh, listening to communications, injecting malicious commands, or disabling devices. The security of Z-Wave has improved in recent versions, but earlier generations are still in widespread use and often contain known vulnerabilities.

In larger IoT ecosystems, especially those involving industrial control systems (ICS), protocols like Modbus and BACnet are commonly used. These protocols were originally designed decades ago, long before cybersecurity was a concern. As a result, they lack any form of encryption, authentication, or integrity checking. When these protocols are used over IP networks in modern deployments, they become easy targets for attackers who can spoof commands, replay traffic, or manipulate device behavior. While secure alternatives such as Modbus Secure or BACnet Secure Connect have been introduced, their adoption remains slow due to compatibility concerns, device limitations, and cost factors. Without protocol upgrades or protective layers like VPNs and firewalls, these environments remain highly vulnerable.

One of the significant complications in securing IoT protocols is the heterogeneity of the devices and networks involved. IoT systems often consist of devices from multiple manufacturers, each implementing protocol standards in slightly different ways. This lack of uniformity makes it difficult to enforce consistent security policies across the ecosystem. Additionally, many devices are deployed in the field for years without receiving firmware updates, which means vulnerabilities discovered after deployment often remain unpatched indefinitely. Even when security protocols are implemented, weak configurations such as the use of self-signed certificates, lack of mutual authentication, or poor key management severely reduce their effectiveness.

To address protocol security holistically in IoT environments, device identity and mutual authentication must be prioritized. Protocols such as the Lightweight Machine-to-Machine (LwM2M) protocol and the use of Public Key Infrastructure (PKI) offer ways to assign unique identities to devices and ensure that only authorized entities can communicate with one another. LwM2M supports secure bootstrap mechanisms and can use DTLS to establish trust. However, like many secure protocols, its success depends on correct and complete implementation. Automating the provisioning of device certificates, rotating keys regularly, and using hardware security modules (HSMs) or trusted platform modules (TPMs) for key storage are necessary to strengthen the cryptographic foundation of these protocols.

Another emerging solution involves the use of secure tunneling and overlay networks that encapsulate insecure protocols within encrypted channels. For example, VPN tunnels, secure proxies, or encrypted message queues can wrap insecure IoT protocol traffic in a secure transport layer. This approach does not fix the protocol itself but adds a shield around it. However, it introduces latency and overhead, which must be balanced against the performance requirements of the IoT system. Real-time systems such as industrial automation or smart grids require deterministic performance, so any added security measures must be optimized for speed and reliability.

Monitoring and intrusion detection are also key to securing IoT protocols. Behavioral analysis tools can monitor protocol traffic patterns and flag anomalies such as unusual device communication, traffic spikes, or unauthorized commands. Because many IoT protocols use fixed command sets and predictable traffic flows, deviations from normal behavior are easier to identify. Logging, telemetry, and real-time alerting can provide insights into potential security breaches, misconfigurations, or compromised devices. Integrating these tools with centralized security platforms or Security Operations Centers (SOCs) enhances the visibility and management of protocol security in IoT deployments.

In securing communication protocols across IoT environments, collaboration between hardware manufacturers, protocol developers, and security experts is essential. Standardization efforts must continue to prioritize security as a core component rather than an optional feature. Security-by-design principles, where devices and protocols are built with security in mind from the beginning, are critical for achieving long-term resilience. Only by treating protocol security as a foundational pillar of IoT system design can organizations hope to deploy safe, reliable, and trustworthy networks in an increasingly connected world.

Certificate Management and PKI

Certificate management and Public Key Infrastructure (PKI) are fundamental components of modern cybersecurity frameworks, providing the backbone for secure communications, identity verification, and data integrity across digital systems. As networks, applications, and devices become increasingly interconnected, ensuring that entities can trust each other is more important than ever. PKI enables this trust by using digital certificates to authenticate users, systems, and services while ensuring that the data exchanged between them is encrypted and cannot be tampered with. However, the true strength of PKI lies not only in the cryptographic principles it employs but also in the efficient and secure management of digital certificates throughout their lifecycle.

A digital certificate acts as a digital passport for entities within a network. It binds a public key to an identity, such as a person, device, or organization, and is issued by a trusted Certificate Authority (CA). This certificate includes information such as the subject's identity, the public key, the issuing CA's identity, the expiration date, and a digital signature from the CA. The digital signature assures that the certificate has not been altered and that it was indeed issued by a trusted entity. When a certificate is presented during a handshake or transaction, the recipient can validate it using the CA's public key and establish a secure, authenticated connection.

The process of issuing, renewing, revoking, and managing these certificates is what defines certificate management. Poor certificate management can lead to severe consequences, including expired certificates that disrupt services, compromised keys that lead to data breaches, and the inability to revoke certificates that are no longer trusted. Organizations must have robust processes and tools in place to ensure that certificates are properly tracked, maintained, and rotated according to policy. This is especially critical in environments where hundreds or even thousands of certificates are in use across servers, containers, mobile devices, and embedded systems.

At the core of PKI is the Certificate Authority, which is responsible for issuing and validating certificates. There are two main types of CAs: root and intermediate. A root CA is the topmost trusted authority in the hierarchy and is used to sign the certificates of intermediate CAs. These intermediate CAs, in turn, issue certificates to end entities. This chain of trust minimizes risk by keeping the root CA offline or heavily protected, while day-to-day operations are handled by intermediates. Trust in the PKI system depends on the integrity of this hierarchy, and any compromise of a CA can lead to widespread trust issues.

Equally important to issuance is certificate revocation. Sometimes, a certificate must be invalidated before its expiration date, such as when a private key is compromised or a certificate was issued in error. PKI provides mechanisms like Certificate Revocation Lists (CRLs) and the Online Certificate Status Protocol (OCSP) to handle this. CRLs are periodically updated lists published by CAs that contain serial numbers of revoked certificates. OCSP, on the other hand, allows real-time verification of a certificate's status. While both mechanisms are useful, OCSP provides more up-to-date information and is often preferred in environments where timely revocation is essential.

In the modern enterprise, automation is a key component of effective certificate management. Manual processes are too slow and error-prone to keep up with the dynamic needs of cloud services, microservices, and DevOps pipelines. Automated certificate management systems can integrate with DevOps tools to automatically request, install, and renew certificates without human intervention. They can also provide visibility into certificate usage, alert administrators before expiration, and enforce policies on key length, certificate duration, and trusted CAs. This reduces the risk of service outages caused by expired certificates and ensures compliance with internal and regulatory standards.

Public Key Infrastructure is not only used in server-to-server communication but is also essential in securing end-user interactions. Web browsers rely on PKI to verify that the website a user is visiting is legitimate and has not been spoofed. When a browser connects to a site using HTTPS, it checks the site's certificate against a list of trusted root certificates. If the certificate is valid and matches the domain, the browser establishes a secure, encrypted connection. If the certificate is invalid or not trusted, the browser warns the user and may block access. This simple yet powerful mechanism is one of the most visible uses of PKI and underscores its importance in establishing digital trust.

In addition to internet browsing, PKI is widely used in securing email communications through protocols like S/MIME. By signing emails with a digital certificate, the sender can prove their identity and ensure that the contents of the message have not been altered. Recipients can also encrypt their replies using the sender's public key, ensuring that only the intended recipient can read the message. This is particularly important in corporate and government communications where confidentiality and authenticity are paramount.

IoT devices also benefit from PKI. Each device can be provisioned with a certificate during manufacturing or onboarding, which allows it to authenticate itself securely when connecting to networks or services. This approach scales well in large deployments, such as smart cities or industrial systems, where traditional authentication methods are not feasible. By using mutual TLS, devices can verify each other's identity, and secure communication can be established even over public or untrusted networks.

Mobile and remote work environments further highlight the importance of certificate management. Employees working from various locations and using different devices require secure access to corporate resources. VPNs and remote access solutions often rely on certificates for authentication, eliminating the need for passwords and reducing the risk of phishing attacks. Certificates can also be integrated into mobile device management solutions to ensure that only compliant, registered devices are allowed to connect, enhancing the overall security posture of the organization.

Despite its many benefits, PKI also introduces certain challenges. Managing trust across different domains, handling certificate expiration, preventing misuse of trusted certificates, and ensuring compatibility across platforms all require careful planning and execution. Organizations must invest in PKI governance, defining clear roles and responsibilities, maintaining secure infrastructure for CAs, and performing regular audits to ensure compliance and readiness.

Certificate management and PKI represent a foundational layer of cybersecurity, enabling encrypted communications, digital signatures, and trusted identities across diverse systems. Their effectiveness depends not only on the strength of cryptographic algorithms but on disciplined lifecycle management, proper automation, and vigilant oversight. In a world where digital interactions continue to grow in volume and complexity, mastering certificate management and PKI is essential for maintaining the confidentiality, integrity, and trustworthiness of every connection.

Analyzing Network Traffic with Wireshark

Analyzing network traffic with Wireshark is a fundamental skill for cybersecurity professionals, network administrators, and anyone involved in diagnosing or securing computer networks. Wireshark is a powerful, open-source network protocol analyzer that allows users to capture and interactively browse the traffic running on a computer network. By using Wireshark, users can inspect the data traveling through their network at a granular level, from high-level protocols down to individual bytes of a data stream. This capability makes it invaluable for troubleshooting, security investigations, protocol development, and learning how networks operate.

Wireshark operates by capturing packets, the basic units of data transferred over a network. Each packet contains not only the actual data being transferred but also important metadata such as source and destination IP addresses, protocol headers, port numbers, and flags that determine how the data should be processed. When Wireshark captures these packets, it presents them in a human-readable format that breaks down the various layers of each packet according to the OSI model. Users can see Ethernet frame details, IP packet structure, TCP or UDP segments, and the application-level payload, all within an intuitive graphical interface.

One of the most valuable features of Wireshark is its deep protocol analysis. It supports hundreds of different network protocols, from standard ones like HTTP, DNS, and TCP/IP to more specialized or proprietary ones used in industrial control systems or telecommunication networks. Wireshark decodes the packets and presents the content in a structured tree view, allowing users to drill down into each protocol layer. For example, when analyzing an HTTPS session, Wireshark shows the TLS handshake details, cipher suite negotiation, certificate exchange, and session key establishment. This level of detail is critical for understanding how protocols behave and identifying anomalies or misconfigurations.

Capturing traffic with Wireshark can be done in several ways. The most common method is to run Wireshark on a machine connected to the network and use its interface to select a network adapter for live packet capture. In some cases, especially in switched networks, capturing all traffic may require the use of port mirroring on switches or network taps to ensure visibility into packets not directly addressed to the capturing device. For remote environments, packet captures can be collected using command-line tools like tcpdump and imported into Wireshark later for detailed analysis. This flexibility makes Wireshark suitable for both real-time monitoring and offline forensic investigations.

Filtering is essential when working with large packet captures, and Wireshark provides a robust filtering language to help users focus on specific traffic. Display filters can isolate traffic by IP address, port, protocol, packet length, or even specific fields within protocol headers. For instance, a filter like tcp.port == 443 would show only traffic using TCP port 443, typically used for HTTPS. Filters can be combined using logical operators to narrow the view to very specific interactions, such as traffic between two hosts using a particular protocol during a defined time window. These capabilities are critical when analyzing network problems or identifying suspicious activity in a large dataset.

Wireshark also allows users to follow a TCP or UDP stream, which reconstructs an entire conversation between two endpoints. This is especially useful when investigating application issues or security events, as it presents the entire communication flow in order, making it easier to understand what data was exchanged and whether it deviated from expected behavior. For instance, following a TCP stream might reveal a failed authentication attempt, unexpected data transfers, or application-level errors. In cybersecurity investigations, such analysis helps in reconstructing attack sequences or data exfiltration attempts.

In addition to protocol analysis, Wireshark includes tools for statistical analysis of network traffic. Users can generate summaries of protocol usage, top talkers by bandwidth, or communication endpoints. This overview can help detect abnormal patterns, such as a spike in traffic to unknown destinations, which may indicate malware activity or a misconfigured device flooding the network. Graphs of packet sizes and frequency over time can also help identify denial-of-service attacks, retransmissions due to network congestion, or performance bottlenecks. These statistical views complement the packet-level analysis by providing broader context to the traffic being examined.

Security professionals often use Wireshark to detect evidence of malicious activity on a network. Unusual protocol behavior, connections to known bad IP addresses, malformed packets, or the use of outdated or insecure protocols can all be indicators of compromise. Wireshark's ability to inspect packet payloads allows analysts to spot patterns or keywords related to malware or command-and-control traffic. In some cases, it can even be used to reconstruct files transferred over the network, such as documents sent over HTTP or FTP, providing direct evidence of data leakage. However, such capabilities must be used ethically and in compliance with organizational policies and privacy laws.

Wireshark is also an excellent educational tool. For students of networking and cybersecurity, it provides a visual, hands-on way to understand how data moves through a network. Observing the behavior of different protocols in real time, inspecting how handshakes are performed, and watching how errors like packet loss or fragmentation affect communication builds a deep understanding of network fundamentals. This experiential learning is far more effective than reading about protocols in theory and helps build intuition for diagnosing and securing real-world systems.

Despite its strengths, using Wireshark requires caution. Because it captures all traffic visible to the selected network interface, it can collect sensitive data, including passwords, private messages, and authentication tokens, if the traffic is not encrypted. Therefore, Wireshark should be used responsibly, and access to it should be restricted to authorized personnel. Capturing traffic on networks without proper permission may violate privacy laws or organizational policies. To ensure ethical usage, Wireshark includes capture filters and data redaction features that allow users to focus only on necessary traffic and avoid collecting more information than required.

Wireshark's extensibility and active community have made it a continuously evolving tool. New protocol dissectors, plugins, and scripts are regularly developed to expand its capabilities and support emerging technologies. This ensures that Wireshark remains relevant as networking protocols evolve and new challenges arise in traffic analysis. Whether used for debugging network issues, performing security audits, teaching networking concepts, or conducting incident response investigations, Wireshark remains one of the most trusted and powerful tools available for understanding and securing network communication at a fundamental level.

Hardening Protocol Implementations

Hardening protocol implementations is a critical process in strengthening the security posture of any system that communicates over a network. Protocols define the rules by which data is transmitted between devices and services, but the real-world implementations of these protocols often vary and are prone to vulnerabilities. A protocol may be secure in theory, but poor coding practices, outdated libraries, or misconfigurations can leave systems exposed to exploitation. Attackers frequently target these weak implementations to bypass authentication, inject malicious commands, or exfiltrate data. As such, it is essential for developers, administrators, and security professionals to understand the importance of hardening protocol implementations and take a systematic approach to securing them.

One of the most common issues in protocol implementations arises from incorrect handling of input. Network protocols are designed to accept data from external sources, which makes them natural targets for malformed or malicious input. Buffer overflows, injection flaws, and unexpected data types can all cause unintended behavior if not properly sanitized. To harden a protocol implementation, developers must implement strict input validation routines that account for every possible edge case. Parsing routines should be designed defensively, assuming that any data received from the network may be hostile. Fuzz testing, which involves feeding randomized or malformed input to a program, is a powerful technique for uncovering weaknesses in parsers and protocol handlers before attackers do.

Insecure default configurations are another frequent weakness in protocol implementations. Many software packages ship with permissive settings that prioritize usability or backward compatibility over security. Features such as anonymous access, deprecated ciphers, or verbose error messages can unintentionally provide attackers with opportunities to compromise a system. Hardening protocols requires reviewing and changing default settings to enforce strong security policies. For example, disabling support for outdated SSL versions, enabling strict certificate validation, or enforcing rate limits on authentication attempts are all steps that improve the resilience of a protocol implementation.

Authentication mechanisms within protocol implementations are often targeted by attackers seeking to impersonate legitimate users or systems. Weak password policies, lack of multifactor authentication, or improperly stored credentials can all lead to compromise. When implementing a protocol that includes authentication, such as SSH, HTTP, or RADIUS, it is essential to use strong cryptographic methods and secure storage for secrets. Passwords should be hashed using slow, salted algorithms such as bcrypt or scrypt, and wherever possible, authentication should rely on asymmetric key pairs or token-based methods. Additionally, protocols should enforce account lockouts, logging, and alerting to detect and respond to unauthorized access attempts.

Encryption is central to secure protocol implementations, but the choice of algorithms and key management practices plays a decisive role in their effectiveness. It is not enough to simply enable encryption; the protocols must use strong, well-reviewed cryptographic primitives and enforce minimum key lengths. Outdated algorithms like RC4 or MD5 should be disabled entirely, as they are no longer secure against modern attacks. Proper implementation of TLS, for instance, requires selecting robust cipher suites, enforcing forward secrecy, and avoiding fallback mechanisms that allow downgrade attacks. Certificate validation must also be implemented correctly, verifying the full chain of trust and checking for certificate revocation using mechanisms like OCSP or CRLs.

Protocol hardening also involves minimizing the protocol's attack surface. Every feature, extension, or open port represents a potential vector for attack. Features not in use should be disabled, and unnecessary services should not be exposed. For example, if a server supports both HTTP and FTP but FTP is not needed, it should be disabled entirely. Network segmentation and firewall rules can further reduce the exposure of protocol implementations by limiting which clients can access certain services. By adopting a principle of least privilege, systems can reduce the opportunities available to attackers and contain breaches more effectively if they occur.

Monitoring and logging are crucial for detecting anomalies and responding to attacks against protocol implementations. Every request, response, and error message can offer insight into how a protocol is being used or abused. Protocol-specific logging should include timestamps, source IPs, request types, and error codes to help identify suspicious activity. These logs should be centralized and correlated with other security events to provide comprehensive visibility. Implementing intrusion detection and prevention systems that understand protocol behavior can help detect attacks such as command injection, brute-force attempts, or protocol tunneling.

Patch management is another essential element of hardening protocol implementations. Vulnerabilities in protocol libraries and daemons are regularly discovered, and attackers are often quick to exploit systems that have not been updated. Keeping protocol implementations up to date with the latest security patches is one of the most effective ways to prevent exploitation. This includes operating system updates, library upgrades, and firmware patches for embedded devices. Where possible, automated update systems should be employed, but care must be taken to test updates in staging environments to prevent unintended service disruptions.

Protocols designed for internal networks often lack security features under the assumption that the internal environment is trusted. This assumption no longer holds in modern environments where threats may originate from within the network itself. Implementations of internal protocols should be reviewed with the same scrutiny as internet-facing services. For example, protocols like SMB or SNMP have been historically exploited due to weak authentication and lack of encryption. Hardening these implementations involves enforcing strong access controls, encrypting traffic, and disabling legacy versions that lack security features.

In containerized and cloud-native environments, protocols are implemented at many layers, from application-level APIs to service mesh communication. Here, protocol hardening must extend to ensuring secure service discovery, API authentication, and secure inter-container traffic. Using mutual TLS within service meshes, enforcing RBAC for service endpoints, and rate limiting API access are all ways to harden protocol implementations in these dynamic ecosystems. Container security scanning tools can detect known vulnerabilities in protocol libraries and flag configurations that expose insecure services.

Testing and validation are ongoing responsibilities in protocol security. Implementations must be subjected to regular penetration testing, code reviews, and security audits to identify flaws that automated tools may miss. Protocol behavior should be verified not only under normal operating conditions but also under stress, invalid input, and network anomalies. Regression testing ensures that fixes do not reintroduce old vulnerabilities or create new ones. By integrating security testing into the development lifecycle, organizations can identify and mitigate protocol-related issues early, reducing the risk of exploitation in production environments.

Hardening protocol implementations requires a multi-layered approach that combines secure coding, strict configurations, continuous monitoring, and timely updates. As attackers evolve their techniques and target increasingly complex systems, the robustness of protocol implementations becomes a primary line of defense. Whether securing communications between servers, clients, devices, or microservices, ensuring that protocol implementations are resilient, compliant, and monitored is essential for maintaining the security and stability of digital infrastructure.

Security Protocol Standards and Compliance

Security protocol standards and compliance form the structural foundation of cybersecurity in modern digital environments. As organizations increasingly rely on interconnected systems, cloud services, mobile platforms, and remote access, the demand for consistent, reliable, and standardized security protocols has never been greater. These standards ensure that data is transmitted, stored, and accessed in a secure manner, regardless of the technology stack or geography involved. At the same time, compliance with these standards is not just a technical obligation but a legal and regulatory requirement for many organizations, especially those operating in sensitive or highly regulated industries such as finance, healthcare, and critical infrastructure.

Security protocol standards are formal specifications that define how different components of an information system should communicate securely. These protocols cover a wide range of functions including authentication, encryption, integrity verification, and secure communication. For instance, the Transport Layer Security (TLS) protocol is the de facto standard for encrypting data in transit across the internet, protecting everything from online banking sessions to corporate email communications. TLS ensures that data cannot be intercepted or altered by unauthorized parties, and it does so through a well-defined process of cryptographic handshake, key exchange, and certificate validation. Standards like TLS are developed and maintained by international organizations such as the Internet Engineering Task Force (IETF), which coordinates the creation of protocols that are open, interoperable, and widely accepted.

Another widely adopted protocol standard is the Secure/Multipurpose Internet Mail Extensions (S/MIME), which provides end-to-end encryption and digital signing of email messages. It allows organizations to ensure the authenticity and confidentiality of their internal and external communications. In enterprise environments, S/MIME is often integrated with Public Key Infrastructure (PKI) systems that manage certificates and keys. Similarly, standards like IPsec are used to secure IP communications by authenticating and encrypting each IP packet in a communication session. These protocols are particularly important in virtual private networks (VPNs), where secure connections must be maintained across untrusted networks.

Identity and access management protocols such as OAuth 2.0, OpenID Connect, and SAML (Security Assertion Markup Language) also play a vital role in standardizing how users and systems authenticate and authorize one another. OAuth 2.0 enables secure token-based access without requiring the user to share credentials with every service. OpenID Connect extends OAuth to include authentication, allowing single sign-on across platforms. SAML, though older, is still extensively used in enterprise environments to facilitate federated identity across different organizations and services. These protocols reduce the risk of password-related breaches and enable fine-grained access control based on roles, context, and behavior.

Compliance with security protocol standards is essential for organizations to demonstrate due diligence and adherence to industry regulations. Frameworks such as the Payment Card Industry Data Security Standard (PCI DSS), the Health Insurance Portability and Accountability Act (HIPAA), the General Data Protection Regulation (GDPR), and ISO/IEC 27001 require the use of secure protocols for data protection. PCI DSS, for instance, mandates that organizations handling credit card data must use strong encryption methods like TLS 1.2 or higher to protect cardholder data during transmission over open, public networks. HIPAA requires healthcare providers and their business associates to use secure methods to protect electronic protected health information (ePHI), including when it is transmitted between systems or organizations.

Achieving compliance is not simply a matter of implementing protocols; it requires organizations to prove that those implementations meet the required standards and are consistently applied. This involves documentation, auditing, monitoring, and sometimes third-party assessments. For example, organizations may be required to maintain logs of encryption certificate expirations, conduct regular vulnerability scans to ensure outdated protocols are not in use, or produce reports showing that only approved cipher suites are enabled in their systems. Security misconfigurations, such as allowing deprecated SSL versions or using weak hashing algorithms, can lead to noncompliance and expose organizations to legal and reputational risks.

Standardization of protocols also promotes interoperability between different vendors and platforms. In complex IT environments that combine legacy systems with modern cloud infrastructure, the ability to communicate securely and seamlessly is vital. By adhering to recognized security standards, organizations ensure that different systems can exchange data securely without requiring custom, proprietary solutions that are harder to manage and audit. This is especially important for multinational corporations and government agencies that must operate across jurisdictions with varying legal and technical landscapes.

Security protocol standards are not static. They evolve to respond to emerging threats, vulnerabilities, and advancements in computing. As such, compliance is a continuous process that requires organizations to stay updated on protocol deprecations and new best practices. For instance, older versions of TLS, such as TLS 1.0 and 1.1, have been deprecated due to known weaknesses and should no longer be used. Organizations that fail to upgrade their systems accordingly not only fall out of compliance but also expose themselves to potential exploits. Staying compliant thus involves patching, reconfiguring, and sometimes rearchitecting systems to adopt newer, safer protocols.

Another important aspect of protocol standardization and compliance is the concept of policy enforcement. Many organizations implement security policies that mandate the use of certain protocols under specific conditions. These policies are enforced through configuration management tools, security gateways, and automated compliance scanners. For example, a policy may require that all internal API calls use mutual TLS, or that all remote access must be tunneled through

IPsec VPNs. Security orchestration platforms help enforce these policies at scale and provide real-time alerts when violations are detected.

Vendor support for standardized security protocols is also a key consideration. When choosing software, hardware, or cloud service providers, organizations must evaluate whether the vendor's products support required security protocols and compliance features. This includes checking for secure default configurations, availability of audit logs, support for certificate management, and compatibility with identity federation standards. Failure to choose compliant and secure vendors can compromise the organization's entire security posture and make achieving compliance more difficult.

Security protocol standards and compliance efforts ultimately contribute to the trustworthiness of digital infrastructure. They provide assurance to customers, partners, regulators, and internal stakeholders that data is being handled responsibly and that risks are being actively managed. As cyber threats continue to grow in scale and complexity, the consistent application of secure communication protocols and strict compliance with evolving standards remain among the most effective strategies for protecting sensitive information and ensuring the resilience of digital systems.

Future Trends in Network Security Protocols

Future trends in network security protocols are being shaped by the rapid evolution of technology, the expanding threat landscape, and the growing demands of privacy, scalability, and performance. As digital transformation continues across all sectors, the networks that connect people, devices, and data must become not only faster and more efficient, but also significantly more secure. Traditional security protocols, while foundational, are increasingly challenged by new attack vectors, quantum computing prospects, and decentralized systems. This dynamic environment is driving the development and adoption of innovative protocols and enhancements that will define the future of secure communications.

One of the most significant trends in network security protocols is the widespread adoption of encryption by default. In the past, many network services operated in plaintext or used optional encryption only for sensitive transactions. Today, encryption is becoming a baseline requirement, not an exception. Protocols such as TLS 1.3 exemplify this shift, offering faster handshakes, improved privacy, and removal of outdated cryptographic algorithms. TLS 1.3 reduces the attack surface by eliminating support for weak cipher suites and forward secrecy is mandatory, ensuring that past communications remain secure even if long-term keys are compromised. In the future, even more application-layer protocols are expected to embed strong encryption by default, making it harder for attackers to intercept or manipulate traffic.

Post-quantum cryptography is another major area influencing future protocol development. Quantum computers, once fully realized, will be capable of breaking current public key cryptographic algorithms such as RSA and ECC, which underpin most existing secure protocols. This threat has prompted research into quantum-resistant algorithms that can withstand such attacks. The National Institute of Standards and Technology (NIST) is currently leading efforts to standardize post-quantum cryptographic schemes, and future security protocols will need to incorporate these new primitives to ensure long-term confidentiality. As a result, hybrid protocols that combine classical and quantum-resistant encryption are expected to emerge, providing a transitional path while quantum technology continues to develop.

Another important trend is the rise of zero-trust networking models, which are influencing how protocols are designed and deployed. Traditional perimeter-based security is giving way to architectures where trust is never assumed, and every interaction is verified. This requires protocols to support continuous authentication, fine-grained access control, and context-aware policy enforcement. Protocols such as OAuth 2.1, OpenID Connect, and new identity-based frameworks are evolving to provide richer metadata, support dynamic authorization decisions, and reduce reliance on static credentials. Similarly, transport protocols are being adapted to integrate with service meshes and microsegmentation strategies, ensuring secure service-to-service communication in dynamic, cloud-native environments.

Decentralization is also driving innovation in security protocols. As blockchain and distributed ledger technologies gain traction, the need for decentralized identity and trust mechanisms becomes more urgent. Decentralized Identifiers (DIDs) and Verifiable Credentials (VCs) represent a shift away from centralized certificate authorities and federated identity models. In future networks, users and devices may present cryptographically signed credentials issued by multiple, independent entities. These credentials can be verified without relying on a central authority, reducing the risk of single points of failure or compromise. Security protocols will need to support these decentralized authentication flows and handle revocation, expiration, and delegation in a distributed and trustless environment.

Privacy-preserving protocols are gaining attention as regulatory pressures and consumer expectations increase. With data privacy becoming a key concern, future security protocols must minimize the amount of metadata exposed during communications. Encrypted DNS protocols like DNS over HTTPS (DoH) and DNS over TLS (DoT) are already reducing visibility into user queries from unauthorized observers. Encrypted Client Hello (ECH), an extension to TLS, seeks to hide the destination server name from network intermediaries during the handshake, addressing one of the last pieces of unprotected metadata in HTTPS connections. As these protocols mature, they will contribute to a more private internet by default, making surveillance and profiling more difficult for attackers and unauthorized entities.

Automation and machine learning will also influence how future protocols operate. With network complexity increasing, it becomes unrealistic for humans to manually configure and manage every aspect of protocol deployment. Adaptive protocols that can adjust encryption levels, routing paths, or authentication mechanisms based on real-time risk assessment are on the horizon. These intelligent protocols could use telemetry and behavioral analysis to dynamically reconfigure themselves, avoid suspicious endpoints, or isolate compromised devices without disrupting legitimate traffic. Such capabilities will be critical for implementing proactive, rather than reactive, security strategies in highly dynamic environments.

Protocol agility, or the ability to easily switch between or upgrade cryptographic algorithms and protocol versions, is becoming a design priority. In the past, many systems were built with hardcoded protocol stacks that were difficult to update, resulting in prolonged exposure to vulnerabilities. Future security protocols are being designed with agility in mind, allowing administrators to update cipher suites, key lengths, and protocol components without replacing entire systems or disrupting services. This modular approach ensures that systems can rapidly adapt to new threats and cryptographic advancements, reducing the window of vulnerability and supporting long-term sustainability.

In cloud-native and edge computing environments, protocols must also account for the ephemeral and distributed nature of workloads. Services may scale up or down rapidly, migrate between data centers, or operate in disconnected states. Security protocols must support seamless identity verification, key distribution, and secure data transport across these changing conditions. Technologies like SPIFFE (Secure Production Identity Framework for Everyone) and SPIRE (SPIFFE Runtime Environment) are emerging to address these challenges, providing a uniform identity layer for microservices and workloads regardless of where they run. These frameworks are expected to be integrated into future network protocols to ensure consistent security across heterogeneous infrastructures.

Finally, standardization and global collaboration will remain essential for the successful evolution of network security protocols. Open standards developed by organizations like the IETF, ISO, and NIST provide the foundation for interoperability, auditability, and trust across borders and industries. As new threats emerge and technologies evolve, these bodies must continue to adapt, ensuring that protocols are both secure and implementable in real-world systems. Industry-specific initiatives, such as those for industrial IoT, automotive networks, and healthcare systems, will also need to develop domain-specific protocols that balance security with operational constraints like latency, power consumption, and legacy compatibility.

The future of network security protocols lies in adaptability, privacy, quantum resistance, and decentralization. As networks become more complex and critical to everyday life, the protocols that secure them must evolve to meet new challenges. This evolution requires not only technological innovation but also a cultural shift toward proactive, standardized, and resilient approaches to security. The coming years will see a convergence of disciplines—cryptography, artificial intelligence, systems engineering, and policy—to create protocols that are not only technically sound but also capable of defending against the increasingly sophisticated threats of the digital age.

Case Studies in Protocol Implementation

Examining real-world case studies in protocol implementation provides invaluable insights into the challenges, successes, and lessons learned in the field of network security. Protocols are the fundamental building blocks of communication in digital systems, and their implementation is a complex process that involves far more than simply following technical specifications. When implemented correctly, protocols provide a reliable and secure foundation for operations. However, history has shown that flaws in protocol implementation—whether due to poor design choices, misinterpretation of standards, or insufficient testing—can have devastating consequences. These case studies highlight both the technical intricacies and the organizational decisions that shape the security outcomes of protocol deployments.

One of the most famous examples of a flawed protocol implementation is the Heartbleed vulnerability in OpenSSL, disclosed in 2014. OpenSSL is an open-source cryptographic library widely used to implement TLS, the protocol that secures much of the internet. Heartbleed was the result of a simple coding oversight in the implementation of the TLS heartbeat extension. The vulnerability allowed attackers to send a malformed heartbeat request that tricked the server into responding with data from its memory, potentially including private keys, usernames, passwords, and other sensitive information. What made Heartbleed especially dangerous was the ease of exploitation and the wide reach of OpenSSL, which was embedded in millions of web servers, routers, and embedded systems. The incident highlighted the critical need for thorough code review, fuzz testing, and strong governance in the development of widely-used security libraries.

Another instructive case is the KRACK attack, discovered in 2017, which exploited weaknesses in the WPA2 protocol used to secure Wi-Fi networks. KRACK, which stands for Key Reinstallation Attack, did not stem from a failure in the design of the WPA2 protocol itself, but rather from how it was implemented in many client devices. During the four-way handshake used to establish encryption keys, KRACK allowed an attacker to replay and manipulate handshake messages, forcing the client to reinstall an already-in-use key. This reinstallation reset associated parameters like the packet nonce, enabling replay attacks and potentially allowing decryption of traffic. The case of KRACK revealed the importance of adhering not just to protocol specifications but to their security assumptions, especially when implementing cryptographic procedures on client devices. It also underscored the vulnerability of IoT devices and smartphones, many of which took months or years to receive necessary patches.

TLS protocol implementations have also provided numerous case studies. One such example is the POODLE attack, which took advantage of SSL 3.0 fallback mechanisms still supported by many TLS implementations. Although SSL 3.0 was considered obsolete and insecure, some servers and browsers continued to support it for compatibility reasons. Attackers were able to downgrade secure connections to SSL 3.0 and then exploit vulnerabilities in its block cipher mode to decrypt sensitive data. POODLE exposed the dangers of backward compatibility in protocol implementations and led to a push for more aggressive deprecation of outdated protocols and cipher suites. It also illustrated the need for implementation strategies that fail safely rather than allowing insecure fallbacks.

Beyond cryptographic protocols, implementation challenges have also emerged in industrial control systems and SCADA environments. One such case involved the Modbus protocol, which was never designed with security in mind. In one widely analyzed deployment, a water treatment facility was found to be using Modbus over TCP without any form of encryption or authentication. An attacker with access to the network could send Modbus commands to change chemical dosing levels, disable alarms, or shut down systems entirely. This case emphasized the danger of directly exposing legacy protocols in modern, IP-based networks and the critical importance of using secure tunnels, firewalls, and access control mechanisms when integrating such protocols into current infrastructures.

In the realm of mobile communication, the implementation of the Signaling System 7 (SS7) protocol has been a source of persistent vulnerabilities. SS7 was designed in the 1970s for routing calls and text messages between telephone networks. It lacks authentication mechanisms, making it possible for attackers with SS7 access to track users' locations, intercept calls and texts, or even redirect authentication messages used in two-factor authentication systems. Real-world breaches exploiting SS7 have been reported, including thefts from bank accounts that relied on SMS for verification. The SS7 case illustrates the long-term consequences of implementing protocols without foresight into modern threat models and the challenge of securing telecommunications infrastructure that was never intended to be exposed to hostile actors.

A more recent and positive example of protocol implementation can be found in the deployment of QUIC, a new transport layer protocol developed by Google and now standardized by the IETF. QUIC integrates TLS directly into the transport layer and operates over UDP, offering both performance improvements and security benefits. From its inception, QUIC was designed with strong cryptographic protections, connection migration capabilities, and resistance to several classes of attacks common in TCP-based protocols. The implementation of QUIC in web browsers and content delivery networks has shown how new protocols can be deployed at scale while prioritizing security, provided that there is close collaboration between protocol designers, implementers, and standards bodies.

The adoption of encrypted DNS protocols, such as DNS over HTTPS (DoH) and DNS over TLS (DoT), also provides instructive case studies. While these protocols enhance privacy by encrypting DNS queries, their implementation has raised new operational and policy challenges. For instance, when browsers implemented DoH by default, network administrators found their traditional DNS filtering mechanisms bypassed. This led to friction between privacy advocates and enterprise security teams, illustrating the complexities that can arise even when protocols are implemented securely. A successful protocol deployment must consider not only technical correctness but also the broader ecosystem, including user expectations, administrative controls, and compliance requirements.

These case studies collectively demonstrate that protocol implementation is a nuanced discipline that demands careful attention to detail, rigorous testing, and continuous monitoring. Mistakes in implementation can undermine even the most secure protocol designs, while thoughtful, forward-looking deployments can set new standards for both security and usability. From the initial design phase through to widespread adoption, collaboration between developers, security researchers, and system architects is essential to ensure that protocols fulfill their intended purpose without introducing new risks. Ultimately, these real-world examples serve as both cautionary tales and models for future best practices in protocol security.

Conclusion and Best Practices

The effective design, implementation, and management of security protocols are essential to safeguarding digital infrastructure in an increasingly complex and interconnected world. Network security does not depend on a single tool or a one-time configuration but on a continuous, layered strategy built upon well-established principles, standards, and practices. Security protocols, when properly implemented, provide the critical foundation for authentication, confidentiality, integrity, and non-repudiation in digital communications. However, the effectiveness of these protocols relies not only on their theoretical soundness but also on how they are deployed, maintained, and adapted to evolving threats.

One of the most important practices in securing protocols is rigorous adherence to current standards. Organizations must rely on protocols that are actively maintained, widely supported, and developed through open, peer-reviewed processes. Choosing secure versions of protocols, such as TLS 1.3 over deprecated versions like SSL 3.0 or TLS 1.0, is not optional but mandatory for maintaining a resilient security posture.

When legacy systems require compatibility with outdated protocols, mitigation strategies such as network isolation, access control, and segmentation must be enforced to minimize risk. Relying on up-to-date protocol standards ensures that known vulnerabilities are addressed and that systems are compatible with modern cryptographic best practices.

Cryptographic hygiene remains central to the secure operation of any protocol. Organizations must enforce strong key management policies that include proper generation, distribution, storage, rotation, and revocation of cryptographic keys. Public Key Infrastructure must be managed with the utmost care, ensuring that certificate authorities are trusted, certificates are valid and not expired, and all participants in a secure exchange can verify each other's identities with confidence. Automation plays a significant role here, reducing the chances of human error and making it feasible to maintain certificates across a large number of services and systems. Weak keys, misconfigured certificates, and expired credentials are often the root cause of major security incidents that could have been easily avoided through disciplined management.

Comprehensive testing of protocol implementations is essential for detecting flaws before they can be exploited. Developers should subject all protocol code to static analysis, dynamic testing, and formal verification when applicable. Fuzz testing, in particular, is a powerful method for uncovering edge-case vulnerabilities that traditional testing might miss. Security researchers have found countless bugs in widely used implementations simply by feeding them malformed or unexpected inputs. All protocol implementations should be designed with secure coding principles in mind, favoring simplicity, input validation, and defense in depth. Reviewing open-source components for security updates and integrating them properly is also crucial, as dependencies often introduce risk if not maintained and monitored.

Operational best practices must include continuous monitoring, logging, and alerting related to protocol activity. Systems should be configured to generate logs for connection attempts, authentication events, failed negotiations, and certificate validation errors. These logs should be centralized and analyzed in real time to detect signs of misuse, anomalous behavior, or compromise. Advanced threat

176

detection tools, such as intrusion detection systems and machine learning-based anomaly detection, can help identify protocol-based attacks like scanning, spoofing, or session hijacking. Real-time visibility into protocol behavior enables faster incident response and helps ensure that the controls in place are working as intended.

Another key principle is the minimization of the attack surface. Protocols and services that are not needed should be disabled entirely, and those that are required should be limited to the minimum number of ports, endpoints, and features necessary. By reducing the number of exposed services and interactions, organizations make it significantly more difficult for attackers to find exploitable vectors. Firewalls, access control lists, and segmentation should be used to restrict protocol traffic to known and authorized systems. For example, administrative protocols like SSH or RDP should never be accessible from the open internet and should be protected with multi-factor authentication and monitored continuously.

The integration of secure protocols into cloud environments requires additional considerations. In dynamic, distributed environments, protocols must support elasticity, microservices communication, and workload mobility while maintaining end-to-end security guarantees. Tools like service meshes, identity-aware proxies, and automated certificate management are vital to ensure that every service interaction is authenticated and encrypted. Cloud-native protocols and APIs must be subjected to the same level of scrutiny and testing as traditional protocols, and configurations must follow secure defaults. DevOps teams must work closely with security professionals to embed protocol hardening into infrastructure as code and continuous integration pipelines.

Awareness and education are also critical components of best practices in protocol security. Organizations should train their development, operations, and security teams to understand how protocols work, what their common pitfalls are, and how to detect and mitigate attacks that target them. Security is not a one-time event but a shared responsibility that requires ongoing learning, practice, and adaptation. Creating a culture where secure communication practices are understood and valued can significantly reduce the risk of protocol-related vulnerabilities.

Collaboration with the wider community, including participation in standards development, threat intelligence sharing, and responsible disclosure programs, further enhances protocol security. Many of the most severe vulnerabilities in protocol implementations have been discovered and reported by third-party researchers, ethical hackers, and academic teams. Encouraging transparency, open discussion, and peer review accelerates the discovery of flaws and improves the overall quality of protocol design and deployment. Public disclosure, when handled responsibly, leads to better awareness, faster patching, and stronger defenses across the industry.

Protocol security also benefits greatly from regular audits and compliance checks. Independent assessments by internal teams or external auditors provide a fresh perspective and help uncover overlooked misconfigurations or inconsistencies. These reviews should include not just the protocols themselves but the policies, procedures, and documentation that govern their use. Aligning with industry frameworks and regulatory requirements such as ISO 27001, NIST Cybersecurity Framework, or sector-specific guidelines ensures that protocol implementations are not only technically sound but also legally and operationally compliant.

Maintaining secure protocols in a rapidly evolving threat landscape demands vigilance, discipline, and a proactive mindset. From cryptographic agility and certificate lifecycle management to secure configuration and monitoring, each layer of defense contributes to the overall resilience of digital communication. By following best practices, staying aligned with emerging standards, and investing in education and collaboration, organizations can effectively protect their networks and data, ensuring that the protocols underpinning our digital world continue to serve as a stronghold against compromise.

www.ingramcontent.com/pod-product-compliance
Lightning Source LLC
LaVergne TN
LVHW051236050326
832903LV00028B/2430